SPIRITUAL DANGERS *of the* 21ˢᵀ CENTURY

REV. JOSEPH M. ESPER

D1082300

Queenship

PUBLISHING COMPANY

P.O. Box 220 • Goleta, CA 93116

(800) 647-9882 • (805) 692-0043 • Fax: (805) 967-5133

www.queenship.org

RESCRIPT

In accord with canon 827§2-3 of the *Code of Canon Law*, I hereby grant ecclesiastical approval for the publication of a book entitled *Spiritual Dangers of the 21st Century* by Reverend Joseph M. Esper.

Given at Detroit, Michigan, on the memorial of St. Isaac Jogues and St. John de Brébeuf, priests and martyrs, and their companions, martyrs, this nineteenth day of October, in the year of our Lord, two thousand nine.

The Most Reverend Allen H. Vigneron
Archbishop of Detroit

Notary

Library of Congress Number # 2009940662

Published by:
    Queenship Publishing
    P.O. Box 220
    Goleta, CA 93116
    (800) 647-9882 • (805) 692-0043 • Fax: (805) 967-5133
    www.queenship.org

Printed in the United States of America

ISBN: 978-1-57918-381-6

Table of Contents

Introduction

The great Russian author Leo Tolstoy began his novel *Anna Karenina* with the words, "Happy families are all alike; every unhappy family is unhappy in its own way."

To a certain extent, this insight also applies to societies and historical ages: the elements of peace, progress, and prosperity are largely similar in each successful civilization or age of widespread contentment (though these "golden eras" of human existence are admittedly unusual, and generally short-lived). Troubled times, however, while sharing some common characteristics, usually involve their own unique crises and challenges; it's as if new tests of character arise to confront and confound the smug sense of superiority possessed by each succeeding generation.

This is certainly the case early in the 21st century. Not only does humanity as a whole (with most Americans definitely included) consider itself more advanced, enlightened, and sophisticated than ever before; the challenges confronting today's world are, in many ways, unprecedented. Rather than looking at such problems as overpopulation and global warming (whether these crises are real or imagined), along with concerns over renewable energy, good stewardship of the earth, health care, the elimination of poverty, the possibility of nuclear terrorism or a global holocaust, and other serious issues of a material, financial, or political nature, the focus of this book is on the realm of the spirit. What specific spiritual dangers confront Catholic Christians as the 21st century enters its second decade?

The Seven Deadly Sins have been alive and well throughout most of human history—but in the Western world, they're now tolerated, and even celebrated, more than ever before. Immorality is nothing new, but the sins of contemporary America (especially in regard to sexual immorality, abortion, and genetic engineering and the scientific manipulation of life itself) might well shame and appall the residents of ancient Sodom and Gomorrah. Religious persecution of (and, unfortunately, sometimes by) Christians is nothing new—but modern technology allows for the surveillance and suppression of believers to an extent previously unimaginable.

No one can yet say with absolute certainty whether our era of Church history is the one which will undergo the scourge of the Antichrist's brief but diabolically horrible reign over the earth; we have every reason to pray and hope we may be spared such a test. It cannot be denied, however, that we face many other tests of a severe and challenging nature.

Never before has human technology been so advanced, and with such a great capacity of being misused or of leading people astray; ever-new and more amazing inventions, scientific discoveries, and medical advances have convinced growing numbers of people that all the secrets of life will eventually be unlocked, obviating the need for a Creator—if indeed, He exists at all. More than any earlier era of history, ours might be called the "Age of Atheism"; even though a majority of Americans still claim to believe in God, increasing numbers of people live in a way that suggests His existence has no meaning for them personally. A practical denial of God, a refusal to abide by divine law, and a rejection of the moral authority of His Church, all underlie such phenomena as societal disintegration, narcissistic leadership, widespread and even violent youthful rebellion, self-destructive forms of entertainment, and cultural degradation.

Christians who take their faith seriously—unless called to a monastic lifestyle—are not supposed to withdraw from such a world, but to transform it; their influence, example, and prayers are intended to demonstrate God's love for the world—a love so great that He sent His only Son for its salvation (cf. Jn. 3:16). Fulfilling this mission, however, requires an awareness of the challenges we face—challenges which, while they can only be overcome through divine grace, require us for our part to be as "shrewd as serpents and simple as doves" (Mt. 10:16).

This book is offered as a possible resource for Catholics seeking to be "salt of the earth" and "light for the world" (cf. Mt. 5:13-14) in early 21st century America. God has blessed our country in unprecedented ways—and much is expected of those to whom much is given (cf. Lk. 12:48). May our efforts to recognize and overcome the unique spiritual dangers and challenges confronting us help bring about a new age of grace for ourselves and our families, our nation, and our Church.

The Moral Disintegration of America

Chapter 1

The Seven Deadly Sins in Today's Society

A middle-aged woman came to her doctor and complained of chronic tiredness and a recent tendency to drop things. "I must be getting old," she said—but as she described her symptoms, the doctor became suspicious: something other than mere aging had to be causing her difficulties. After taking and examining a chest X-ray, he discovered a mass compressing her windpipe. He asked, "Don't you have trouble breathing?" "No," she responded; "I just get tired."

After explaining that her problem seemed to be caused by a lump that had extended into her chest, the doctor scheduled surgery. During the operation, a tumor the size of an orange was discovered and removed; it had actually bent the woman's windpipe, constricting it severely. When the woman later came in for a follow-up visit, she shouted joyfully, "I can breathe! I feel like a teenager again; I can breathe!" As the doctor later noted, "That lump must have been growing slowly for fifteen years or more, gradually compressing her trachea, like a boa constrictor tightening its grip. The woman had adapted without thinking about it."[1]

This story is a good analogy of the deadly effects of sin: it can squeeze the spiritual life out of individuals, and even out of nations and societies, without its victims fully realizing it. Indeed, such a process seems to be far advanced in our own country today; moral standards in the United States have declined to an alarming degree—but most of our fellow citizens seem unconcerned. A number of Christian authors[2] have sounded the alarm, pointing out that we now accept ideas, values, and forms of public expression that would have horrified earlier generations of Americans—but like the proverbial frog in the gradually boiling pot of water, our nation is largely oblivious to the moral dangers that threaten us.

According to the *Catechism of the Catholic Church,*
Sin creates a proclivity to sin; it engenders vice by repetition of the same acts. This results in perverse inclinations which cloud conscience and corrupt the concrete judgment of good and evil (par. 1865).

Following the moral teachings of St. John Cassian and St. Gregory the Great, the Church has identified certain sins as "capital" because they lead to other sins and vices. These particular sins, commonly known as the *Seven Deadly Sins,* are anger, greed, envy, lust, sloth (laziness), gluttony, and pride. Any one of these, left unchecked, can grow to the point where it makes the practice of virtue increasingly difficult, and finally chokes off one's spiritual life completely.

This same process is undeniably at work in American society today; thus, before beginning a more specific study of the spiritual dangers confronting individual religious believers in the United States here in the 21st century, it will be helpful to consider very briefly the influence of each of the Seven Deadly Sins upon a society that was specifically founded as "one nation under God."

Anger

Can anyone deny that America is becoming an increasingly angry society? Granted, we're largely free of the explosive racial and ethnic tensions that afflict much of the world, and most Americans pursue their serious grievances via the legal system, rather than taking the law into their own hands; nevertheless, the United States has become a much more violent place over the last few decades. Another murder occurs in our country every 27 minutes, and a serious crime is committed every three seconds.[3] Also, with less than 5% of the world's population, our country has almost one-quarter of the world's prisoners—a total of 2.3 million criminals behind bars.[4] Even though society has a duty to lock up those who are willing to inflict violence on others, the fact that our prison population is so large can be seen as an alarming indication of an underlying state of anger, and a lack of self-control and a respect for others, permeating American culture.

Furthermore, the National Institute of Mental Health has noted that over 7% of U.S. adults—some 16 million people—will experience some form of a rage disorder (with such terms as "road rage," "desk rage," and even "vending machine madness" entering common language).[5] Many people today take offense very easily, while others constantly nurse grievances, real or imagined (often encouraged by politicians and community activists with a personal stake in fomenting social resentments and class warfare). Our court system is overwhelmed with civil suits, even though many of these cases could easily be resolved if the parties involved were willing to discuss their differences reasonably. Also, anger in the home often leads to troubled marriages, divorce, teenage rebellion, and various other problems destructive of families and of society.

When Our Lord taught, "Whoever is angry with his brother will be liable to judgment" (Mt. 5:22), He was referring specifically to individuals—but His words also apply equally to nations and societies (for numerous Old Testament passages speak of the Lord being angry not only at individual sinners, but with His people as a whole). Moreover, St. James warns us that "everyone should be quick to hear, slow to speak, slow to wrath, for the wrath of a man does not accomplish the righteousness of God" (1:19-20).

Greed

Stories of corporate greed and corruption, Wall Street bailouts, gigantic bonuses and "golden parachutes" for undeserving CEOs, hugely overpaid entertainers and athletes, and similar instances of economic injustice, no longer surprise the average American; as citizens of "America, Inc." we've almost become inured to such events. However, as members of a consumer society, and as part of what is simultaneously the richest—and most indebted—nation in history, few of us are completely untouched by the lavish lifestyles and acquisitive attitudes that have come to characterize the United States of the early 21st century.

For many Americans, money is practically worshipped as a god, even though Scripture warns that "the love of money is the root of all evils" (1 Tim. 6:10). Conspicuous consumption seems to be the American way, and the desire for continued material progress—which can be legitimate in itself—is often perverted into a yearning for ever more economic benefits and blessings, even as much of the world remains mired in poverty. It is true that America is the greatest producer in human history of material prosperity—not only for itself, but for many other nations, as well—and Americans have traditionally been very generous (at least those who hold more traditional political and moral values[6]). However, the lures of material prosperity have certainly seduced and ensnared many, if not the majority, of our fellow citizens—and as Jesus warns, "no one can serve two masters" (Mt. 6:24).

God's plan in giving America unprecedented freedom and prosperity was to have her as a leader and example to the rest of the world, and for much of our nation's history, this plan was more or less fulfilled. However, our God-given blessings have become like the golden calf that led the Israelites astray (cf. Ex. 32)—and because the Lord is a jealous God (cf. Ex.20:5; Dt. 4:24), His judgment upon our greed will one day surely come.

Envy

Envy violates the Tenth Commandment, and is defined in the *Catechism* as "sadness at the sight of another's goods and the immoderate desire to acquire them for oneself" (par. 2539). In some ways America is less envious than many other nations, for rarely in her history has she sought to expand her borders through military conquest, and frequently her foreign policy has sought peace, or at least stability, in troubled areas of the world—unlike traditional imperial powers seeking to gain or enhance their "place in the sun" by diplomatic maneuvering and the threat of war. Also, as a wealthy nation, the United States has less reason to be envious than most other countries in the world today.

Nevertheless, envy is a powerful force in our society. The admirable freedom to create one's own destiny and wealth, and the widespread experience of upward mobility in our country's history (the so-called "American dream"), has, in recent times, been overemphasized and even perverted into a constant imperative to "keep up with the Joneses" by acquiring the latest technological devices—especially in the fields of communication and entertainment. Contemporary advertising relies upon envy as a key tool in convincing us that we need all sorts of new products, services, and experiences; young people in particular are targeted in this manner. Moreover, increasing numbers of Americans have a sense of entitlement—that is, the conviction that the world owes them a living, that no limits should be imposed upon their potential choices, and that their happiness should be guaranteed.

According to St. James, "if you harbor bitter envy and selfish ambition in your hearts, do not boast about it or deny the truth. Such 'wisdom' does not come down from heaven but is earthly, unspiritual, of the devil. For where you have envy and selfish ambition, there you find disorder and every evil practice" (3:14-16). Those who believe this danger applies only to individuals might note the words of St. Clement of Rome from late in the 1st century: "Jealousy and strife have overthrown great cities and uprooted mighty nations" (*First Epistle to the Corinthians,* par. 6).

Lust

America's sins against the Sixth Commandment need very little elaboration here (and, in fact, some important aspects of this subject will be covered in greater detail in Chapter 3). Suffice it to say that sexual immorality is rampant, several million unmarried couples live together, millions of Americans suffer from sexually-transmitted diseases, the use of contraception is widespread (bringing in its wake all the evils Pope Paul VI warned of in his 1968 encyclical *Humanae Vitae*[7]), pornography has become a multi-billion dollar industry (destroying many marriages and families in the process), the promotion of "gay rights" by the homosexual movement has become more blatant and aggressive than ever before,[8] and well over 50 million innocent, unborn children have been murdered in the womb following the 1973 U.S. Supreme Court decision which invalidated virtually all legal restrictions on abortion.

Various alleged private revelations have claimed that abortion and homosexual behavior are the two sins in American culture today most offensive to God; if this is true (and there seems to be no good reason to doubt it), then our society—like that of ancient Babylon (cf. Dn. 5:25-27) will surely be tried and found wanting.

Sloth

Compared to people of many other lands and nations, Americans have always had a reputation as being hard-workers, and in some ways that's still true today. The average American works more hours, and is more productive, than his or her European counter-part, and U.S. society as a whole is constantly reinventing, rebuilding, and reestablishing itself. America is a remarkably busy and vibrant nation—but that doesn't mean sloth isn't a danger.

Sloth refers to the sin of spiritual and moral laziness—and in our nation today, this sin is especially linked to the worship of leisure and entertainment. Many Americans live for the weekend—not to attend church, but to play golf, watch sporting events on TV, engage in hobbies, take part in family outings, or drive their children to various tournaments and competitions. Needless to say, all these activities mean that people are "too busy" or "too tired" to worship God each week as part of a faith community. Quite frequently, the sincere and consistent religious and moral upbringing of children also falls by the wayside—to the point where even many *Christians* in America believe that the main significance of the holidays of Christmas and Easter is that families have the opportunity to spend time together.[9]

Furthermore, a growing underclass in our nation has been corrupted by the "welfare mentality," in which it becomes increasingly difficult—or even repugnant—for disadvantaged persons to take responsibility for their own material and spiritual well-being. For many people, hard work has become something to avoid as much as possible. Even among industrious citizens, affluence frequently leads to spiritual apathy, and labor-saving devices and techniques often result ultimately in moral laziness. Our society's "worship of leisure" clearly violates God's injunction in the First Commandment not to have other gods than Him (cf. Ex. 20:3). Like the ancient Romans whose preoccupation with bread and circuses blinded them to reality, more than a few Americans today are spiritually and morally lazy—and thus risk sharing the fate of the unfaithful servant severely punished for neglecting his duty (cf. Mt. 24:45-51).

Gluttony

Obesity is a huge and growing concern in the United States: over 25% of all Americans are heavily overweight (compared to about 18% in 1998), and it's estimated this problem costs our nation almost $147 billion per year in medical and other expenses.[10] Some of the problem is due, of course, to our relatively sedentary life-styles and the consumption of much processed, sugar-laden foods; however, there can be no denying the fact that many Americans eat much more than necessary (while also wasting large amounts of food). An obsession with eating is also reflected in our nation's spending priorities. In 1999, for instance, Americans spent $13 bil-lion on chocolates, $58 billion on soft drinks, and $110 billion on fast-food restaurants (but donated only $2.9 billion to their churches to use in missionary work and evangelization).[11]

Our affluence, coupled with modern agricultural techniques, has given average Americans more food, of more varieties, than virtually any other society in history (though without completely eliminating hunger in our nation). For most people in past ages (and for a billion or more people in the world today), the sin of gluttony wasn't a physical possibility—but that's not the case here in the United States today. An even greater sin is committed, however, by those who deliberately ignore the needs of starving or malnourished people—whether around the world, or on their own doorstep. Our Lord's parable of the rich man and Lazarus (Lk. 16:19-31) warns us of the grave danger of indulging ourselves while neglecting the poor among us.

Pride

In her more than 230 years of existence, the United States has had many amazing and historically unprecedented accomplish-ments; we as Americans can rightly be very proud of our nation's history and achievements. However, a justifiable patriotic pride can easily degenerate into spiritually-corrosive arrogance. Signs of this were prevalent after the 9-11 attacks; the slogan "God bless America" could be seen and heard everywhere. Due to our sense of national entitlement, however, these words often seemed to be more of a demand than a prayer—as if we were naturally entitled to God's blessings and protection, in spite of our continued flouting of His commandments.

Our nation's rising tide of immorality, exploitation of the poor, economic injustices, rejection of traditional sexual morality, growing celebration of homosexuality, genetic experimentation and even the manipulation of the elements of life itself, exaltation of science and technology at the expense of human dignity, and, above all, massive assault on human life in the womb, all constitute an increasingly brazen moral rebellion and a rejection of divine law. Every historical civilization that has traveled such a path has eventually collapsed—but we smugly assume that somehow America is exempt from such a fate. Our wealth, our military might, and our technology will, in the minds of so many of our fellow citizens, allow us to continue in our hedonistic lifestyle without worry or interruption.

Even though the United States contains much good and still serves, in many ways, as a beacon of light and freedom for the world, and even though many millions of Americans still desire to live as part of "one nation under God," the growing arrogance of our cultural, political, and economic leaders—along with the spiritual apathy and complacency of much of our population—almost assures a severe imposition of divine justice. Jesus warns that those who exalt themselves will be humbled (Lk. 14:11). If America must be brought to her knees to be reminded of her need for God, the Lord, in His justice *and mercy*, will have no alternative but to exercise a painful judgment upon our land.

Thus, a brief examination of America's moral state, using the criteria of the Seven Deadly Sins, gives us much reason for alarm; our nation, blessed by God more richly than any other in history, has fallen far short of her founding ideals. All is not lost; millions of our fellow citizens yearn for a return to traditional morality, and, through divine grace, a vast spiritual renewal is possible. The Lord assures us that "if My people, upon whom My Name has been pronounced, humble themselves and pray, and seek My presence and turn away from their evil ways, I will hear them from Heaven and pardon their sins and revive their land" (2 Chr.

7:14). Each of us is called to pray, sacrifice, and work for such a result—but even as we do this, we must be aware of the spiritual dangers that threaten each of us as individuals. To some degree, we will each share in the blessings, or judgment, that comes upon our land—but it is as individuals that we will one day stand before God to give an account of our lives.

NOTES

[1]Paul Brand, *In His Image* (Zondervan, 1984), pp. 176-177.

[2]See, for instance, David Kupelian's *The Marketing of Evil: How Radicals, Elitists, and Pseudo-Experts Sell Us Corruption Disguised as Freedom* (WND Books, 2005).

[3]Fr. Bill McCarthy, MSA, *God Bless America—God's Vision or Ours?* (Queenship Publishing, 2003), pp. 78-79.

[4]"US Prison Population Dwarfs that of Other Nations," *International Herald Tribune*, April 23, 2008 (www.globalresearch.ca).

[5]"Count to Ten: How to Cope With Anger," *Christopher News Note #517.*

[6]A study by the non-partisan Catalogue for Philanthropy analyzed state-by-state charitable giving for 2004, and developed a "Generosity Index" which ranked all fifty states by giving as a percentage of household income. The top twenty-five charitable states by this measure were all "red states" (meaning those more politically conservative). Furthermore, Syracuse University professor Arthur Brooks, in his 2006 book *Who Really Cares? America's Charity Divide: Who Gives, Who Doesn't, and Why It Matters,* states, "Conservative households in America donate 30 percent more money to charity each year than liberal households," and "Religious people are 21 percent more likely to volunteer in explicitly secular causes" [than liberals].

[7]Paul VI warned explicitly of likelihood that the widespread use of contraception, or birth control, would lead to increased marital infidelity, a general lowering of morality in society, a loss of respect on the part of men for women, and the use of coercive methods by governments to control population growth (cf. *Humanae Vitae*, n. 17).

[8]In his article "The Selling of Gayness in America" (*The Priest*, July 2009), Father Val J. Peter notes that the gay movement is attempting to impose its agenda not merely through traditional political means, but by persuading—indeed, conditioning—Americans to accept and even celebrate the gay lifestyle. A key element in this process is something called "exaction pricing," which means making opponents of the gay agenda pay a severe price for their oppo-

sition—e.g., portraying them as bigots, ridiculing them in public (as happened to Dr. Laura Schlessinger), and defining the expression of traditional Christian morality (especially Scriptural condemnations of homosexual activity) as "hate speech."

[9]McCarthy, *God Bless America*, op. cit. p. 72.

[10]"Health Buzz: Obesity Costing America Billions," *U.S. News & World Report*, July 29, 2009 (based on statistics published in the journal *Health Affairs*).

[11]www.emptytomb.org. More recent figures include $22 billion for snack foods (2002), and (in 2007) $12 billion for specialty coffee, $16.8 billion for bottled water, $29 billion for candy, $22 billion for snack foods, and $72 billion for carbonated soft drinks.

Chapter 2

The Remaking
of American Culture

With the exception of nations devastated and defeated in war—such as Germany and Japan in the aftermath of World War II—rarely in history has a country's culture changed so dramatically and in such a short time as has happened in the United States over the last fifty years. For better or for worse, the world in which our parents and grandparents grew up is gone forever.

Some of the changes witnessed by Americans over the age of forty or fifty are truly wonderful and amazing. For instance, the Civil Rights Movement succeeded in altering not only the laws of our country, but also the attitudes of many millions of our fellow citizens; while racism still exists, in terms of bringing about racial equality, America has achieved more progress in a shorter period of time than virtually any other society in history—and we can rightly be proud of this.

Other amazing accomplishments over the last fifty years include victory in the Cold War—without a major military conflict—and the resulting liberation of millions of people; economic progress and the creation of vast amounts of wealth, leading to greatly improved standards of living for most Americans; huge strides in preserving the environment and cleaning up many of the worst effects of pollution; incredible technological developments, including computers, the internet, and cell phones; a much greater sensitivity to the rights and needs of the disabled; and major advances in health care and medicine—many of which would have been literally unthinkable in previous ages. There's no disputing the fact that some of the radical changes we've witnessed are truly worth celebrating.

At the same time, however, compared to the America of fifty years ago, our society is far more violent, coarse, and morally degraded. Much of this decline happened in that tumultuous era of reappraisal and rebellion known as the 1960s. The United States was involved in a highly unpopular war in Viet Nam, and the experience of a Navy pilot named Jeremiah Denton—who later became a U.S. Senator and a political conservative—is instructive.

Denton was shot down over North Viet Nam in 1965 and imprisoned for the next eight years. When he returned to America after being released in 1973, he was shocked to discover, in his own words, "a land of X-rated movies, massage parlors, the new [pornographic] literature on our newsstands, the degree to which our publishing industry had resorted to and favored books and magazines which were decidedly different from what I had seen before. . . ."[1]

Another former Senator, Daniel Moynihan, who as a liberal had expected the 1960s to be a decade manifesting "a spirit of enterprise and daring such that history would look to it as a golden age," instead later wrote that it "progressed from vision to nightmare. The Great Republic had—incredibly, monstrously—been brought to the point of instability."[2]

As one expert noted, liberal democracies such as the United States are subject to radical change more than any other type of society, because their nature depends so much on the character of their citizens,[3] and that character can be fluid and unpredictable. Much of the change in character of Americans over the last fifty years has been highly undesirable; according to David Kupelian in the important book *The Marketing of Evil,*

> As Americans, we've come to tolerate, embrace, and even champion many things that would have horrified our parents' generation: things like abortion-on-demand, judges banning the Ten Commandments from public places, a national explosion of middle-school sex, the slow starvation of the disabled, thousands of homosexuals openly flouting the law and getting "married," and online porn creating late-night sex addicts in millions of middle-

class homes. At the same time, our courts have scrubbed America's schoolrooms surgically clean of every vestige of the religion on which this nation was founded—Christianity. Indeed, in fifty years we've gone from a nation unified by traditional Judeo-Christian values to one in which those same values are increasingly scorned, rejected, and demonized.[4]

American society was battered by a number of traumatic events in the 1960s: the assassinations of President John F. Kennedy, the Rev. Martin Luther King Jr., and Senator Robert Kennedy; the increasingly unpopular Viet Nam War; the Civil Rights Movement, and an angry and sometimes violent backlash; riots; the growing and ever-more visible drug culture; radical changes in music and other expressions of popular culture; and the hippie movement—all of which contributed to, or expressed, a major loss of respect for authority and traditional American values, especially on the part of the young.

According to one sociologist, "If we are looking for a handy phrase to sum up the American cultural revolution of the '60s and early '70s, we can probably do no better than this: *a generalized rebellion against authority.*"[5] Higher education had exposed many young people to the idea that moral values are ultimately only a matter of personal preference. Also, Americans have always believed in "progress," and this theme carried over into the realm of ideas. Because religion and belief in the supernatural are older ideas, many people concluded that the opposite and newer beliefs of secularism and materialism must be better and more useful.[6]

Changing standards in education had a huge effect on American society. Over the last half-century, students in government (that is to say, public) schools have been "indoctrinated into a culture of situation ethics—do whatever it takes to satisfy one's desires in any given situation—while being warned against being discriminatory, judgmental, or intolerant"[7] (i.e., adhering to Judeo-Christian morality). Furthermore, schools took upon themselves the responsibility of "educating the whole child," which in practice meant targeting children's emotions, beliefs, and moral values, instead of merely imparting knowledge.[8]

The rights and duties of parents, along with their competency in raising children, were downplayed by "enlightened" educators who were supposedly dedicated to the overall good of society. Children's values were to be reshaped and made more politically correct by means of subtle manipulation, using techniques such as cognitive dissonance—the process of creating confusion and discomfort by confronting impressionable minds with two conflicting loyalties or beliefs.[9] For example, students' loyalty to the United States was undermined through a long process of criticizing American heroes and values, culminating with the 1996 "National History Standards Project." Instead of emphasizing America's successes and achievements, revised textbooks focused primarily on her sins and failures; also, themes such as disarmament, "peace studies," and the "culture of poverty" were stressed—subtly suggesting that big government must be given the power and resources to solve problems, rather than relying on local institutions and individuals.[10]

At the same time, government schools were failing in their primary mission: providing students with a solid education. For instance, the "whole language" or "look-say" method or reading came into vogue after World War II; this abandonment of traditional phonics prompted the writing of the 1955 bestseller *Why Johnny Can't Read*.[11] Academic standards weren't watered down to the same degree in universities and colleges (America's higher education system remained the finest in the world), but college campuses—in addition to frequently being the seedbed of rioting, rebellion, and other forms of social unrest—became increasingly intolerant not only of religion and traditional viewpoints, but also of a genuinely free exchange of ideas.

The issue of evolution provides a contemporary example of how academic "thought police" attempt to stamp out genuine intellectual diversity. Ben Stein's movie *Expelled* documents numerous cases of highly-respected scientists and educators being ridiculed, denied tenure, and even fired—simply for questioning the validity of the theory of evolution and showing an openness to the possibility of intelligent design. (As a result of the movie, the University of Vermont was pressured into withdrawing its invitation to Stein to serve as a commencement speaker.[12])

Education has also been affected by an emphasis on multiculturalism. On the surface, this might seem reasonable in an increasingly diverse society—but in practice, this trend has little to do with learning any foreign language or culture, and everything to do with the downplaying, or even rejection, of America's Judeo-Christian foundations.[13] Author David Kupelian writes that after the 1960s,

> the various "liberation movements"—sexual liberation, women's liberation, gay liberation, and so on—have blossomed into rampant infidelity, divorce and family breakdown, gender confusion, AIDS, abortion, and other mammoth problems. Moreover, the multicultural madness that started in the '60s has infused virtually all of American society with unending confusion.[14]

Some citizens might look to politics and to the government to address these issues—but, to paraphrase President Ronald Reagan, government itself has become a big part of the problem. (Indeed, governments tend to love crises and problems, for they provide excuses and opportunities for them to increase their authority and control over society.) The size of the federal government is always expanding—often at the expense of state and local authorities, and almost always at the expense of individual liberty. Federal bureaucrats constantly add new (and usually onerous and expensive) regulations, government spending continually rises (harming the overall national economy in the process), and many judges have completely abandoned the concept of judicial restraint.

Moreover, urged on by the news media and groups such as the ACLU (American Civil Liberties Union), the government has set itself up as the arbiter of social and cultural values (an example being so-called "hate crimes" legislation)—in the process often treating religion as, in the words of one commentator, "the enemy of the secular order rather than its basis."[15]

At the same time, crime has skyrocketed over the last fifty years, with children and young people—especially those trapped in inner city schools—frequent witnesses to or victims of violence. These tragedies are more or less reported accurately by journalists, but on many other issues the new media—rather than providing objective coverage—oftentimes question or impugn traditional beliefs and values, while actively working to support political movements and candidates who meet their standards of political correctness.[16]

In many significant ways, the United States is not the same nation it once was. A dramatic change in a society's culture isn't always a bad thing (as in the de-nazification of Germany after World War II). In this instance, it may well prove to be a moral and spiritual disaster—for America is in danger of losing not only her history and her identity, but also her soul.

NOTES

[1]Alan C. Carlson, "On Parents, Children, and the Nation State," in *Whose Values? The Battle for Morality in Pluralistic America*, ed. by Carl Horn (Servant Books, 1985), pp. 59-60.

[2]*Ibid.*, p. 60.

[3]Angelo M. Codevilla, *The Character of Nations* (Basic Books, 1997), pp. 62-63.

[4]David Kupelian, *The Marketing of Evil* (WND Books, 2005), p. 11.

[5]David Carlin, *The Decline & Fall of the Catholic Church in America* (Sophia Institute Press, 2003), p. 67.

[6]*Ibid.*, p. 141.

[7]Gus R. Stelzer, *The State Against Religion: The Case for Equal Protection* (Acorn Press, 2001), p. 49.

[8]B. K. Eakman, *Cloning of the American Mind* (Huntington House, 1998), p. 28.

[9]*Ibid.*, p. 202.

[10]*Ibid.*, pp. 212-213; 222.

[11]Kupelian, op.cit. p. 161.

[12]*Catholic Family News,* March 2009, p. 27.

[13]Codevilla, op.cit. p. 281.

[14]Kupelian, op.cit. p. 89.

[15]Codevilla, op.cit. p. 65.

[16]Kupelian, op.cit. p. 186. The media's blatant and unmistakable bias in favor of Barack Obama during the 2008 presidential campaign (along with its incredibly vicious attacks on Sarah Palin) provide a particularly striking illustration of this point.

Chapter 3

The Rise and Celebration
of Immorality

If we wanted to pinpoint a specific year in which American society took a terrible turn for the worse, many would choose 1973, when the U.S. Supreme Court overturned all restrictions on abortion, resulting in a holocaust that has claimed over fifty million innocent victims so far. Our nation is undoubtedly paying a heavy price for this Supreme Court decision. Not only is our "culture of death" aborting its own soul in a moral and spiritual sense; the economic and social costs of abortion are also staggering[1] (and, as noted earlier, it's said that abortion is one of the sins most offensive to God).

Others might point to 1962 as a decisive year, for it was then that the U.S. Supreme Court, in its *Engel v. Vitale* decision, struck down all laws allowing prayer and Bible reading in government schools (a ruling expanded upon in the following year by the Court's decisions in *Murray v. Curlett* and *Abington v. Schempp*). As a result of these decisions, many millions of students and teachers were prevented from continuing to engage in religious activities that had always been part of the public education system from the earliest days of our nation.[2] Coincidentally or otherwise, educational standards have declined markedly since 1962, while school violence and other serious misbehavior have risen substantially.[3]

However, perhaps the most pivotal year in shaping contemporary American society was 1948—for in that year a zoologist at Indiana University, Alfred C. Kinsey, released his book *Sexual Behavior in the Human Male*. This blatant piece of propaganda foisted a number of dangerous and destructive myths on our nation, including the claims that most American males were—either actually or potentially—sex offenders; that homosexuals comprise as much as 10% of the population; and that children are sexual from birth. Not only are these claims false, but in order to create the statistical tables supposedly corroborating them, Kinsey actually encouraged pedophiles to sexually violate hundreds of infants and children to obtain the fraudulent data he needed.[4]

The truth about Kinsey's highly unethical and illegal methods didn't become widely known until 1981—and by then the damage was done: Kinsey had been acclaimed as the "father of the sexual revolution," and his so-called "research" contributed to a widespread breakdown in American sexual mores. For instance, the Model Penal Code of 1955 relaxed "sexual psychopath" laws—even though society as a whole wanted, if anything, such laws to be tightened—largely because of Kinsey's influence.[5] Also, in 1973 the American Psychiatric Association removed homosexuality from its list of mental disorders—in part because of persuasion (or, more accurately, intimidation) from the gay rights movement; Kinsey's inflated claims on the percentage of homosexuals in America's population gave the movement cultural influence out of proportion to its actual membership.

Today government schools teach—or, more accurately, brainwash—children as young as five years old that homosexuality is "normal," and that to disagree with this statement is a form of hatred. At the same time, sexual immorality is rampant, and because of widespread adultery and fornication, over 50 million Americans suffer from some type of sexually transmitted disease.[6] AIDS has become a politically protected illness; rather than acknowledging the self-destructive nature of the gay lifestyle, the gay rights movement—aided by groups such as the ACLU[7]—insist upon disproportionate federal funding in the search for a "cure."

For Christians, of course, the key issue is abortion, in which innocent human lives are at stake. Even our opponents regard abortion as the key, however, for the simple reason that if so-called "abortion rights" are lost, the entire sexual revolution is in jeopardy—for no matter how readily available contraception might be, there's always the danger of an unwanted pregnancy . . . and if abortion isn't available as a last resort, there really isn't any "sexual freedom."[8] That's why abortion proponents fight tooth and nail against even the most limited restrictions (such as parental notification and informed consent measures), and against attempts to limit such barbaric practices as partial-birth abortion; it's also the reason some politicians with few genuine core beliefs are absolutely uncompromising on this one issue.

Because Americans at first largely saw abortion as a grave moral evil, it was necessary for the abortion industry and its supporters to lie about this topic, to concentrate on "hard cases," and to reframe the subject as one of "choice"—thus gradually creating a political climate allowing the U. S. Supreme Court to issue its *Roe v. Wade* decision in 1973. Former abortionist Dr. Bernard Nathanson, who is now a pro-life Catholic, has testified about his own role in this devious process.[9]

The sexual revolution has had a terrible effect on marriage and on the family. Many children are now raised in homes without a resident father, and numerous studies have shown a strong link between this situation and increased levels of crime, substance abuse, unwed pregnancy, suicide, and other social pathologies. Government programs, rather than solving this problem, often make it worse (and, in fact, the breakdown of the family actually allows the government to increase its influence and power[10]).

According to author Angelo Codevilla, the modern American family

wields less authority over its members and is less important in their lives than ever before. It is smaller because fewer children are born into it, adolescents move out of it sooner, and aged parents seldom move in. And because of divorce, it has a short[er] life expectancy than just one generation ago.[11]

In no other country do parents spend less time with their children than in the United States (with a decline of 40% in just one generation).[12] As a result, many children are growing up "unbonded"—a term meaning young people with no sense of responsibility toward others and no concept of right and wrong. This makes them easy prey to drugs, pornography, gang involvement, and even Satanism; as students, they find it difficult to pay attention or cooperate, and as adults, their attempts at marriage are usually unsuccessful.[13]

This worrying trend also corresponds with a growing rise in narcissism. Experts estimate that 1 out of every 16 Americans (including 1 out of 10 in their twenties) have experienced the symptoms of Narcissistic Personality Disorder,[14] which the Mayo Clinic defines as "a mental disorder in which people have an inflated sense of their own importance and a deep need for admiration."[15] Those suffering from this disorder tend to have a fragile sense of self-worth, making them vulnerable to criticism and incapable of accepting correction. An overemphasis on self-esteem may be a major factor in this growing problem; one child psychologist warns that today's parents and teachers are so "obsessed with praising" young people that they are creating a generation of extremely egotistical children incapable of handling frustration.[16]

Well-known scholar James Q. Wilson has noted that until the mid-1960s, the traditional sources of character-building in our society were the family, the church, the neighborhood, and the school. Today, however, young people are more likely to form their values based on the entertainment industry and their peers—in the process choosing "an ethos that values self-expression over self-control."[17] Even conscientious parents find themselves swimming against the tide. Changing cultural standards—which we might refer to as a form of "moral quicksand"—make it a difficult and ongoing struggle for parents who seek to provide their children with a solid and consistent moral foundation.

Parents must also guard their children from those who would exploit them; that there are forces intent on such exploitation is beyond question. For example, a 2001 PBS documentary called "The Merchants of Cool" exposed how major corporations conduct thorough demographic and sociological studies of young people, and then design advertising around their findings—even to the point of tempting, degrading, and corrupting the target population; moreover, some big corporations actually send spies to young people's social settings in order to gather "marketing" intelligence.[18] Media critic Douglas Rushkoff stated, "Today five enormous companies are responsible for selling nearly all of youth culture. These are the true merchants of cool: Rupert Murdoch's Newscorp, Disney, Viacom, Universal Vivendi, and AOL/Time Warner."[19] (It was Time Warner that marketed a CD called "Cop

Killer" by the rapper Ice-T, enraging police departments across the country; only after actor Charlton Heston embarrassed the company by reading the actual disgusting lyrics at a shareholders' meeting did Time Warner terminate the rapper's contract.[20])

In addition to undermining family life, the entertainment industry has seemingly declared war on Christian values. The Parents' Television Council, or PTC, carefully monitors the growing tide of sex and violence, along with crude and obscene language, found on network and cable TV—especially during what used to be called the "family hour," an evening time slot where producers were careful to avoid programming that might be inappropriate for younger viewers. Respect for family values and sensitivity of this sort are increasingly becoming things of the past; the PTC has noted what appears to be a deliberate attempt to mock traditional values and undermine society's moral foundations.

The same trend is at work in Hollywood. At one time, major studios created biblical blockbusters like *The Ten Commandments* and *Ben Hur*. Nowadays organized religion, and religious characters and values, are routinely ridiculed and disparaged, even though movies taking this route generally make far less money than those respectful of America's religious heritage. Privately financed, wholesome movies like *Bella* and *Fireproof* are largely ignored by the entertainment industry, and when a movie is too big to ignore—like Mel Gibson's *The Passion of the Christ*—it's subject to severe criticism.[21] When it came out in the spring of 2004, columnists issued dire predictions of widespread anti-Semitic violence as a result of the movie—violence which, of course, never happened.

It's no coincidence that vacuous and even self-destructive ideas and behavior—which would have found virtually no adherents in an earlier era of American history—have become very influential, and sometimes even dominant, in contemporary society. Whether we date the decline of our culture from 1948, 1962, or 1973, it cannot be denied that the Judeo-Christian heritage which helped make America the greatest nation in history is now under severe attack, and this trend cannot continue indefinitely. The more God is pushed to the margins of national life, the more the social order begins to unravel—and as average Americans become increasingly uninvolved and unwilling to resist this trend, the more uncertain our nation's future becomes.

NOTES

[1]Dr. Brian Clowes, a researcher for Human Life International (a major pro-life organization), used data from the 2007 Statistical Abstract to estimate the number of persons in various professions lost to U.S. society due to abortion (in other words, what services some of the 50 million victims of abortion would have eventually provided to our nation had they been allowed to live). He calculated that abortion has cost the United States 2 future presidents, 7 Supreme Court justices, 102 U.S. senators, 589 congressmen and women, 8,123 judges, 31 Nobel Prize laureates, 328 Olympic medalists, 6,092 professional athletes, 134,841 surgeons and physicians, 392,500 registered nurses, 1,102,443 teachers, 553,821 truck drivers, 336,939 janitors, 109,984 police officers, and 39,477 firefighters. Moreover, Blessed Mother Teresa of Calcutta is said to have stated that God had already sent into the world the person destined in the future to discover a cure for AIDS, but the world rejected this gift—for this person was murdered in the womb through abortion.

[2]McCarthy, op.cit. pp. 23-24.

[3]Pat Robertson, *The Turning Tide* (Word Publishing, 1993), p. 233. Mr. Robertson refers to statistics presented by David Barton in his book *America, To Pray or Not to Pray* (Wallbuilder Press, 1991), including: SAT scores plunged from 980 in 1963 to 900 in 1990; birthrates of unwed girls (ages 15-19) soared from 15 per 1000 to 35 per 1000; total pregnancies for unwed girls (ages 15-19) leapt from 100,000 in 1963 to 650,000 in 1987; sexually transmitted diseases among teenagers increased from 350 cases per 100,000 to 1200 cases; premarital sex by teenage girls jumped from 23% to 70%; the divorce rate more than doubled from 2.2 per 1000 in 1962 to 4.7 in 1990; single-parent households increased from 4.6 million to 10.9 million; and the incidence of violent crime jumped from 250,000 in 1962 to 1.7 million in 1990.

[4]Kupelian, op.cit. p. 134. See also *The Kinsey Corruption: An Exposé on the Most Influential "Scientist" of Our Time,* by Susan Brinkman (Ascension Press, 2004), pp. 42-43.

[5]Brinkman, op.cit. p. 15.

[6]Robertson, op.cit. p. 22.

[7]F. LaGard Smith, *ACLU: The Devil's Advocate* (Marcon Publishers, 1996), op.cit. p. 109.

[8]Carlin, op.cit. p. 251.

[9]See Bernard N. Nathanson, M. D., *The Hand of God* (Regnery Publishing, 1996).

[10]Kupelian, op.cit. p. 108.

[11]Codevilla, op.cit. p. 266.

[12]Robertson, op.cit. p. 263.

[13]*Ibid.*, p. 175.

[14]David Kupelian, "American Idolatry," *Whistleblower* (May 2009), op.cit. p. 5. According to Jean M. Twenge Ph. D. and W. Keith Campbell Ph. D in "The Narcissism Epidemic: Living in the Age of Entitlement," "the narcissistic culture . . . has drawn in many more. The narcissism epidemic has spread to the culture as a whole. . . . American culture's focus on self-admiration has caused a flight from reality to the land of grandiose fantasy. . . ."

[15]*Ibid.*, p. 4.

[16]*Ibid.*, p. 44.

[17]*Ibid.*, p. 193.

[18]Kupelian, op.cit. pp. 64-65.

[19]*Ibid.*, p. 65.

[20]*Whistleblower,* February 2009, op.cit. p. 25.

[21]David Limbaugh, *Persecution: How Liberals Are Waging War Against Christianity* (Regnery Publishing Inc., 2003), op.cit. p. 289.

Chapter 4

Secularism—
the New National Religion

Jesus warns that those who seek to save their lives will end up losing them, while those who lose their lives for His sake will ultimately find them (Lk. 9:24). The manner in which this truth is being demonstrated most clearly in contemporary America is in the search for personal freedom. The growing rejection of traditional religious and moral values is leading many people astray, with their supposed quest for "authenticity" and "self-actualization" merely leading them—and society as a whole—into a deeper state of spiritual blindness.

One expert notes that the direction of modern society has been that of expanding the area of freedom, or of permissible human behavior, in every area but one: that of religious expression.[1] By deliberately misinterpreting the idea of "separation of church and state" (a phrase which doesn't even appear in the U. S. Constitution) to mean religion must play no public or official role in society, various Supreme Court justices,[2] ACLU lawyers, intellectuals, and other social activists (such as atheist Madalyn Murray O'Hair) have gradually managed to restrict the religious freedom of traditional Christians. This trend has involved not only eliminating prayer from government schools, but denying, as much as possible, the religious principles on which our country was founded. Casting aside the pearl of great price (cf. Mt. 13:46), contemporary American society has created a "marketplace of ideas" in which every conceivable viewpoint is welcome—except that of traditional Christianity.

Back in the 1930s, the Communist theoretician Antonio Gramsci realized that the Western world was too strong to be overcome by Communism at that time—not only because of the West's industrial and economic strength, but especially because of its moral and religious foundations. Communist success, Gramsci taught, would have to come from undermining the Western world from within, gradually manipulating influential members of society to consider every important issue without reference to God, while making organized religion—especially Catholicism—appear as the enemy of human freedom and progress.[3] The success of this long-term project is quite evident in Western Europe, and to a somewhat lesser degree, in the United States—and a central element in this undertaking has been fostering the rise of secularism.

In 1933, educator John Dewey collaborated with some thirty other atheists to write *The Humanist Manifesto*, whose philosophy was eventually enshrined in government schools.[4] Secular humanism rejects the idea of moral absolutes, and proclaims that—even if God exists—human beings are not subject to divine law. Morality is understood solely in terms of situation ethics, which in practice is nothing more than a rationalization allowing one to do virtually whatever one pleases. Under this perspective, "life is experienced as a series of 'breakthroughs' against an oppressive moral order,"[5] and organized religion is seen as irrelevant at best, or, more often, as a set of arbitrary restrictions on human happiness to be rejected and overthrown.

Lacking any solid foundational principles, what we might call the "ethical elasticity" of secularism facilitates logical inconsistencies and even moral hypocrisy—as with the case of supposedly Catholic politicians claiming to be "personally opposed" to abortion, while refusing to do anything that might restrict it in even the slightest degree. Moral schizophrenia is also evident in the fact that the U. S. Supreme Court (in *Torcaso v. Watkins* and *United States v. Seeger*) has declared secular humanism to be a religion—but at the same time, the court system has rejected claims that, as a religion, secular humanism has wrongly been given a privileged place in government schools.[6]

Many people mistakenly assume that secularism is neutral or indifferent to religion, when in fact it has a profoundly negative effect on traditional American moral and religious values. The standard defense secularists offer for their value system—"you choose your moral codes, and we'll choose ours"—sounds reasonable on the surface, but in practice it's a denial and denigration of the Judeo-Christian principles on which our nation was founded. Taken to its logical conclusion, this approach would create a society espousing and defending actions we as Christians are bound to oppose (such as abortion and homosexual "marriage"), while denying us any say in our country's moral values and social policies—in effect allowing secularism to win by default.

While the pseudo-religion of secularism hasn't yet triumphed in America to the same degree it has in Western Europe, its influence is steadily growing—usually at the expense of traditional Christianity. Indeed, by its very nature, secular humanism is anti-Christian (though, of couse, it appreciates and honors "liberal Christians" willing to abandon their values and beliefs for the sake of the latest political movements or social fads).

Christianity in general, and the Catholic Church in particular, upholds unchanging moral principles, especially in the area of sexual morality—thereby earning the disrespect, scorn, or outright hatred of secularists. As the late Pope John Paul II stated, the Church is a "sign of contradiction" to the present age, and so it is frequently ridiculed by the entertainment industry, denounced in popular culture, treated with disdain by the secular media, and sometimes subjected to attempted infringements on its rights (as in legislative acts or judicial rulings requiring Catholic social agencies to facilitate adoption by gays, or to provide employees with health insurance that includes contraceptive coverage).

It would certainly be easier for us to live as dedicated Christians, and undoubtedly much easier to influence our society, if all those who claim to be followers of Christ were genuinely committed to doing His will, regardless of the cost—but unfortunately, that's definitely not the case. Many Christians are religious illiterates, having only the vaguest idea of what the Church teaches.[7] Quite a few others have been seduced by the glamour and materialism of popular society, and are letting themselves be swept along by our culture's changing values.

During his 2008 visit to the United States, Pope Benedict XVI spoke of a "quiet apostasy" among many American Catholics, who—instead of thinking in harmony with the Church—have conformed themselves to the spirit of the age, particularly on issues such as sexual morality, cohabitation, divorce, homosexuality, and abortion. Many Catholics, the Holy Father noted, have also been infected with materialism, secularism, and individualism; as a result, the Church's clear and unchanging teachings have become for them just one opinion among many, rather than the guiding principles of their lives. (Some might trace such a sad state of affairs back to the Protestant revolt of the 16th century, for the logical conclusion of Martin Luther's separation of faith from good works is a bland, shallow, and ineffectual Christianity that has little ability to influence society—let alone its own adherents.[8])

According to Catholic sociologist David Carlin,
> For a long time, we had a balance between talk of freedom (political talk) and talk of order (religious talk). But this balance has been upset, as the religious talk of order—that is, talk of sin and specific virtues and vices—has gone into decline. We still have a vigorous rhetoric of freedom, but we no longer have an equally vigorous rhetoric of order.[9]

He also notes, "Moral liberalism's attack on Christianity is not done by way of violent persecution, but done by way of seduction and ridicule and a certain amount of righteous indignation. . . . And over the last few decades, such methods have worked very well indeed."[10] Conservative Protestants have tried to fight back through such organizations as the American Family Association, the Moral Majority, and Focus on the Family, but Catholics—except for those involved in the pro-life movement or groups such as the Catholic League for Religious and Civil Rights—have been largely absent from the ongoing culture war. This is a serious failure in terms of both religion and citizenship—and it may come with a heavy cost.

Our viewpoint on the dignity and purpose of human life has vast implications; as one author warns,
> The lesson of Nazi Germany is that as soon as a society gets to a point where a majority of its inhabitants accepts the man-as-animal/neurochemical accident view, public policy takes a turn that eventually leads to the nation's downfall or demise. . . . The decisive moment—and there

always is one—was when the average people, whether out of fear, cowardice, anger, or greed, rejected their religious values and began to rationalize and accept justifications for what they knew were wrong.[11]

Furthermore, historians Will and Ariel Durant, in their classic book *The Lessons of History,* concluded, "There is no significant example in history of society successfully maintaining moral life without the aid of religion."[12]

A similar warning is given by the great Russian author Aleksandr Solzhenitsyn, who stated:

Imperceptibly, through decades of gradual erosion, the meaning of life in the West has ceased to be seen as anything more lofty than the "pursuit of happiness". . . . The concepts of good and evil have been ridiculed for several centuries; banished from common use, they have been replaced by political or class considerations of short-lived value. It has become embarrassing to appeal to eternal concepts. . . . Judging by the continuing landslide of concessions made before the eyes of our generation alone, the West is ineluctably slipping toward the abyss.[13]

These are frightening words, but no honest, thinking person can deny their relevance. American society is disintegrating before our eyes, and in all likelihood this trend will continue and intensify.

When St. Peter addressed the crowds in Jerusalem on Pentecost Sunday, he urged them, "Save yourselves from this corrupt generation" (Acts 2:40). He might well give us this same vitally important advice today, for—according to many private revelations—our age is perhaps the most evil and perverse in history.

On Judgment Day, it will not be enough for us to claim, "But I wasn't as bad as most people." God doesn't grade us on a curve; each of us will be held personally and uniquely responsible for what we did or didn't do. One of the great spiritual dangers of our age is the myth that "everybody's doing it, so it must somehow be okay." We have to guard ourselves, and those for whom we're responsible, from this dangerous deception. It is so easy to go along with the crowd, but as Jesus warned, "the gate is wide and the road broad that leads to destruction, and those who enter through it are many" (Mt. 7:13).

Our Lord commands us to let our light shine before all (Mt. 5:16), and even though the darkness of our society hates the light of truth (cf. Jn. 3:19-21), we are called to continue bearing witness to Christ. It's quite possible our example and prayers may help convert someone who would otherwise be lost, but even if this doesn't happen, we still have to be counter-cultural for the sake of our own salvation. God will give us the wisdom, courage, and strength we need to persevere—but the choice is up to us alone: do we want to live primarily as members of this society, or as citizens of the Kingdom of Heaven?

NOTES

[1]James Hitchcock, "Disentangling the Secular Humanism Debate," in Horn, *Whose Values?*, p. 26.

[2]Such as William O. Douglas (d. 1975) and Hugo Black (d. 1971).

[3]Malachi Martin, *The Keys of This Blood* (Simon and Schuster, 1990), pp. 249ff.

[4]Stelzer, op.cit. p. 60.

[5]Hitchcock, op.cit. p. 24.

[6]*Ibid.,* op.cit. p. 30.

[7]Robertson, op.cit. pp. 273-274.

[8]Kupelian, op.cit. p. 239.

[9]Carlin, op.cit. p. 295.

[10]*Ibid.,* op.cit. p. 306.

[11]Eakman, op.cit. p. 408.

[12]Quoted in Stelzer, op.cit. p. 79.

[13]Carl Horn, "'World Views' and Public Policy," in *Whose Values?*, p. 185.

Section B

Technology—
Servant or Master?

Chapter 5

Technological
Benefits and Temptations

We live in the most technologically advanced society of the most rapidly changing era in human history. Experts have stated that the total amount of human knowledge doubles every ten years, and a major portion of this increasing awareness of reality falls within the realm of science and technology.

There are constant discoveries and breakthroughs in the fields of medicine, genetics, engineering, physics, metallurgy, electronics, and numerous other areas. Advances in miniaturization and programming allow computers to do far more than ever before, benefiting—and changing—society in fields as diverse as safety, health care, transportation, robotics, education, finance, law enforcement, communications, and entertainment. Moreover, these trends are likely to continue, and even accelerate, as a result of discoveries and achievements in the fields of nanoscience (the study and manipulation of atomic and molecular-sized particles) and nanotechnology, with particular applications in industrial manufacturing, communications, and medicine.

Over 100 years ago, someone once foolishly speculated that the U. S. Patent Office might just as well be closed, for "everything worth inventing has already been invented." No one would even consider making such a misguided statement today; in fact, there's actually a widespread—though mistaken—expectation that sooner or later some technological answer will be discovered or invented for every problem or inconvenience we human beings face.

Contrary to what many people assume, the Catholic Church is not opposed to human progress and development; indeed, it was the worldview, support (financial and otherwise), and active involvement of Catholicism which helped make scientific progress possible during the last millennium.[1] The Church insists, however, that science is not an end in itself, and that knowledge and progress must not be pursued in a way that compromises human dignity. According to the *Catechism,*

> Science and technology are precious resources when
> placed at the service of man and promote his integral
> development for the benefit of all. By themselves
> however they cannot disclose the meaning of existence
> and of human progress. Science and technology are
> ordered to man, from whom they take their origin and
> development; hence they find in the person and in his
> moral values both evidence of their purpose and
> awareness of their limits (par. 2293).

The great blessings of technology must not blind us to its potential dangers. For instance, family life can be negatively affected; as the late Pope John Paul II warned,

> Thanks to the unprecedented expansion of the commun-
> ications market in recent decades, many families through-
> out the world, even those of quite modest means, now
> have access in their own homes to immense and varied
> media resources. . . . Yet these same media also have the
> capacity to do grave harm to families by presenting an
> inadequate or even deformed outlook on life, on the
> family, on religion, and on morality.[2]

In her book *Noise: How Our Media-Saturated Culture Dominates Lives and Dismantles Families,* author Teresa Tomeo—herself a former broadcast journalist—describes some of the effects technology has upon modern family life:

> E-mail has replaced the personal touch of a handwritten

letter. Children retreat from each other and their families to the privacy of their Game Boys. Teenagers who once congregated on street corners now instant message (IM) from their computers or chat via cell phones. Teens who once gathered in living rooms with their families to watch their favorite TV shows can now catch many of these same prime time programs on their cell phones, anytime and anywhere, thanks to wireless companies. . . .[3]

The front cover of her book contains a quotation from Pope Benedict XVI pointing out one of the spiritual dangers of our age; the Holy Father states, "Put simply, we are no longer able to hear God—there are too many different frequencies filling our ears."

One of the frequencies referred to by Pope Benedict is obviously that of television—and it's long been recognized that excessive TV viewing can have harmful effects, especially upon young people. More than a thousand studies undertaken over the last three decades have shown a connection between simulated violence on TV and in the movies, and aggressive behavior on the part of young people,[4] and the Parents' Television Council stated that television violence has risen by 75% in less than a decade.

The average high school graduate will have seen over 200,000 violent acts on TV, including 16,000 simulated murders—a fact which caused even the self-described liberal atheist Ted Turner (founder of CNN and TBS) to admit, "Television is the single most significant factor contributing to violence in America."[5] TV is also a major factor in the rising tide of sexual immorality among teenagers. A 2004 report by the RAND Corporation (a non-profit research group) found that "sexually-charged television programs definitely influence teens to have sex,"[6] and other studies have shown that young people view as many as 14,000 sexual messages on TV each year (an average of thirty-eight such messages a day).

Besides TV, another very useful—but also potentially dangerous—technological tool is the Internet. It's now accessible not only from computers, but also through wireless networks, cell phones, and PDAs (personal digital assistants). The Internet can be a wonderful resource for research, communications, and entertainment, but it's also loaded with possible temptations and dangers, especially for the young.

Parents and other adults often need to become more aware of what's happening in cyberspace. For instance, there is a number of on-line social networking sites such as Facebook and Twitter; there are also video sharing web sites such as YouTube and MySpace (allowing users to post or upload, view, and share video clips). Photographs of young people in sexually suggestive poses sometimes circulate in this manner (often without the knowledge or consent of the persons involved); it's also becoming more common for teens to send suggestive photographs via cell phones (a phenomenon informally known as "sexting").

Teenagers using social networking sites, or simply chatting on-line with friends (or, in many cases, with unknown persons pretending to be friends) have developed their own codes to circumvent parental supervision. Such abbreviations include PIR ("parent in room"), POS ("parent over shoulder"), ASL ("age, sex, location"), CU ("see you"), and EG ("evil grin"). Even when on-line abbreviations and shortcuts are legitimate, they can contribute to the "dumbing down" of our culture, as slang expressions and loose spelling tend to replace good grammar.

The Internet has many valid uses, but it also involves certain hazards. One obvious danger is, for many people, its addictive nature; some persons—adults included—spend so much time on-line that their relationships, obligations, and even health are negatively affected. Also, on-line pornography is a huge business, generating over $20 billion annually; in 2002, websites peddling pornography and sex were the single largest on-line income generators (exceeding even computer hardware and software sales).[7] Roughly 70% of such on-line activity involving sex and pornography occurs during normal business hours (when employees are supposed to be using the Internet only for work-related purposes), and the word most commonly entered into search engines is "sex." Even more morally disgusting is the existence of some 100,000 websites providing child pornography.[8] Overall, it's estimated that over 200,000 Americans are currently seeking professional help for cybersex addictions.[9]

Young people are no longer emotionally and psychologically safe in their homes; one out of five children in America who regularly use the Internet receive sexual solicitations in Internet chat rooms,[10] and law enforcement agencies estimate that, at any given moment, there are as many as fifty-thousand predators on-line in the United States alone.[11] (Fortunately the FBI and police agencies frequently conduct "sting" operations to capture some of these predators—but by no means has this eliminated the problem.)

In spite of these troubling trends, roughly one-third of American teenagers have Internet access in their bedrooms, allowing them to go on-line without parental supervision. Another serious threat is that of "cyber bullying," in which emotionally vulnerable young people receive taunting or intimidating e-mails; in one case, a teenage girl committed suicide because of constant critical and threatening messages from an on-line bully (who turned out to be the *mother* of one of her classmates).

Video games are another widespread form of technology that can be a legitimate form of entertainment—or a great spiritual and societal menace. The National Institute on Media and the Family estimates that 67% of American households with children own a video game system, and it states that 50% of 4th grade students prefer "first-person shooter video games." These games simulate the use of handheld weaponry (from the perspective of the in-game character); according to the Institute, playing violent video games on a regular basis can increase aggressive thoughts by as much as 43%.[12] Following the 1999 Columbine High School massacre, it was widely reported that the two shooters, Dylan Klebold and Eric Harris, were both hooked on violent video games.

Even when these games are not violent in nature, negative effects are still possible. A study by researchers at Iowa State University found that almost 1 of every 10 children in America, ages 8-18, is actually *addicted* to video games (in the same way that adults can be addicted to alcohol, drugs, or gambling). These "pathological gamers" spend twice as much time playing as other young people (an average of 24 hours per week); they're more likely to be boys, and much more likely to have some form of attention-deficit disorder.[13] Common sense suggests that young people—and adults as well—need adequate time for emotionally healthy activities; thus, an overemphasis on technological forms of entertainment can easily become detrimental to their relationships, obligations, and spiritual development.

It would be illogical, unfair, and mistaken to conclude that technology is a bad thing, and that everyone making extensive use of it is automatically at risk of responding with dangerous, aggressive, unhealthy, or self-destructive behavior. At the same time, however, it cannot be denied that these dangers are real.[14] At the very least, parents must closely monitor their children's interests and activities; ideally, all of us will become more aware of the unique temptations present in our technological society—for even the best and most beneficial inventions can do us grave harm if they undermine our relationship with God.

NOTES

[1]See, for instance, *How the Catholic Church Built Western Civilization,* by Thomas E. Woods, Jr. (Regnery, 2005), pp. 67ff.

[2]Pope John Paul II, World Communications Day 2004, "The Media and the Family: A Risk and a Richness," May 23, 2004.

[3]Teresa Tomeo, *Noise: How Our Media-Saturated Culture Dominates Lives and Dismantles Families* (Ascension Press, 2007), pp. 3-4.

[4]*Ibid.,* op.cit. p. 5.

[5]*Ibid.,* op.cit. p. 63.

[6]*Ibid.,* op.cit. p. 66.

[7]Stephen J. Rossetti, "Internet Pornography: Raising the Alarm," *The Priest* (February 2006), p. 11.

[8]*Ibid.*

[9]Tomeo, op.cit. p. 87.

[10]Rossetti, op.cit. p. 11.

[11]Tomeo, op.cit. p. 84.

[12]*Ibid.,* op.cit. p. 100.

[13]Staci Hupp, "1 in 10 Addicted to Video Games," *The Des Moines Register,* April 20, 2009.

[14]A cautious respect and appreciation for science and technology might be the most prudent and realistic approach for Christians of the early 21st century. This sort of balanced approach is present in a message supposedly given by Jesus to alleged visionary John Leary on September 21, 1994; Our Lord is

reported to have said, "Do not treat science as a god to be worshipped. I have endowed inventors with their ability to help you live a little more easily, but do not abuse your inventions for evil purposes and do not think that science has all the answers of your life. On the contrary, when you gain full knowledge, you will see how little you know and understand. You have only scratched the surface of what can be known."

Chapter 6

A "Brave New World"
in Medicine and Bioethics

In 1932 English author Aldous Huxley wrote a famous novel called *Brave New World*, describing a horrifying future society based on eugenics, test-tube babies, and social engineering. Some of his shocking predictions have come to pass; cloning, genetic experimentation, and other forms of morally-objectionable research are becoming widespread in the United States and elsewhere in the world.

As mentioned earlier, the Catholic Church is not opposed in principle to scientific experimentation and progress, including in the medical field. However, as the *Catechism* states, "Research or experimentation on the human being cannot legitimate acts that are in themselves contrary to the dignity of persons and to the moral law" (par. 2295).

This moral imperative also applies to human embryos, which are required for embryonic stem cell research. The Church teaches that ". . . The body of a human being, from the very first stages of its existence, can never be reduced merely to a group of cells."[1] Furthermore, "The human being is to be respected and treated as a person from the moment of conception. . . ."[2]

Unfortunately, these moral restrictions and safeguards are increasingly ignored by what Pope John Paul II called the "culture of death." Here in the United States, for instance, virtually every state now allows embryonic stem cell research—even though such research requires the destruction of human embryos, and—unlike the morally-acceptable use of adult stem cells—*has yet to discover a single viable cure or treatment for any medical condition.*

In addition to misguided, but perhaps well-meaning, medical

experimentation, some research is apparently being done "just for the hell of it" (in both senses of the term). There was an attempt in Chicago to create hybrid human "she-males" by mixing male and female cells in the same embryo.[3] In India, technicians have been trying to remove rat DNA from rat sperm and replace it with human DNA (for the purpose of using the sperm to impregnate a woman whose husband had a low sperm count).

In England, ovaries have been extracted from aborted baby girls for use in fertility experiments. Also, according to author Michael H. Brown, "in the past [few] years, scientists have created pigs with human blood, fused rabbit eggs with human DNA, and injected human stem cells to make paralyzed mice walk. There are now mice that have human brain cells. . . . There are reports of attempts to create human-pig embryos."[4]

From a Christian perspective, it's hard to deny that humanity is increasingly usurping the rights of the Creator (while perverting His handiwork). The first temptation in recorded history was the serpent's assurance to Eve in the Garden of Eden that "you will become like gods" (Gn. 3:5)—and, of course, Eve's acquiescence opened a Pandora's box of misery and shame for humanity.

According to the realm of private revelation, our world's arrogance is leading us down a similar path today. Two prophecies were allegedly given to an anonymous locutionist fourteen years apart. In December 1990, this person was supposedly told by Heaven that, within four years, mankind would face a decision over a new evil, similar to abortion but not related to it; this temptation would "arrive almost imperceptibly, with few people noticing the depth of its evil, for it will appear to have beneficial and convenient aspects."

Many commentators believe this warning referred to the process of cloning, for in 1994—under changed scientific and legislative conditions—a sheep named "Dolly" was successfully cloned (though it later died of birth defects). On December 22, 2004—just a few days before the terrible tsunami that killed several hundred thousand people—the same locutionist was allegedly told,

There is going to be a major disruption in a region of the world that will affect everyone. The world is now seriously out of conformance with the Will of God and what He created and intended. There are those who would reconfigure the very creatures He has formed, and who meddle with the texture of life. For this reason, the Lord will allow a huge reorientation. If not for the action of Heaven, what God has created on earth will soon be damaged beyond recovery. . . . The event to come will surprise everyone who has offered a prognostication, and will show even recalcitrant scientists, though not all, that there is a fundamental alarm in Heaven over their arrogant and wayward course. Nothing that is artificial in a way that disrupts what God intended will be allowed to stand.[5]

Sister Lucia, one of the Fatima visionaries, related Our Lady's warning that in the second half of the 20th century, many people in society and in the Church—including some Church leaders—would be afflicted with a "diabolical disorientation," making it difficult or impossible for them to tell the difference between right and wrong. One registered nurse, Joanna Swords, has written about how this diabolical disorientation has carried over into the field of health care.[6] We certainly saw evidence of this in the case of Terri Schiavo, whose judicially-mandated execution in 2005 occurred even though she was conscious, alert, and capable of expressing simple responses and emotions (and, contrary to what many claimed, dying by dehydration—the form of death imposed on her—is a terribly prolonged and agonizing way to die).

According to Joanna Swords, doctors and nurses, who are supposed to help save lives, "are also taking lives—by the hundreds of thousands—through abortion, birth control, euthanasia, starvation of patients 'for their own good,' organ donor harvesting, etc."[7] Thus, she says, "we no longer have the assurance that when we enter a hospital or other health care institution . . . our lives will indeed be preserved or that our best interests will be looked after. . . ."[8] For this reason, it is highly advisable to fill out a Health Care Proxy (HCP) form, also referred to as "durable power of attorney for health care." This allows someone of your choice to make decisions for you if you are unable to do so.[9] (Needless to say, it's essential to make sure the person you choose is honest, capable, and fully understands and supports your wishes and moral values;

also, your HCP form should spell out as many of your specific wishes as possible.)

The phrase "death with dignity" is sometimes used to camouflage the murder and disposal of persons considered a burden to society; respect for human dignity and the sanctity of life are being severely eroded in our health care system. A related moral danger threatens health care providers: the elimination of conscience clauses protecting doctors, nurses, and other medical workers from being forced to take part in procedures they consider morally unacceptable.

According to the National Right to Life Committee,

Bias against those who choose not to participate in abortion on moral grounds has been documented for over a decade. In 1996, a case study published in *Issues in Law & Medicine* revealed that applicants for medical school were being screened for their views on abortion, and bias against applicants opposed to abortion was expressed during evaluations for admission. . . . the Christian Medical Association reports that more than 40% of its membership surveyed reported having experienced pressure to violate their convictions, with "physicians . . . losing positions and promotions because of their life-affirming views" and "residents . . . losing training privileges because they refused to do abortions."[10]

In spite of federal laws supposedly protecting health care providers from having to violate their consciences by assisting in abortions,

The increasing national effort on the part of certain groups to employ the coercive powers of state and local government agencies and courts to force health care providers, including religiously affiliated hospitals, to perform or fund abortions is wide-ranging. For example, in Alaska the state supreme court ruled that a community hospital must perform late abortions against the wishes of the hospital's board of directors. Catholic hospitals and HMOs have been pressured by authorities in New Jersey and New York for refusal to provide abortions or abortion-related services. In Connecticut, a certificate of need was denied to a proposed outpatient surgical center because it declined to perform abortions, after abortion activists intervened in the proceedings. A hospital merger in New Hampshire was undone when pro-abortion activists intervened with the state attorney general. The city council of St. Petersburg, Florida, forced a private hospital to leave a non-profit consortium because the consortium followed a pro-life policy.[11]

The Bush Administration had issued a regulation to ensure the conscience rights of health care providers were respected, but soon after Barack Obama's inauguration, his Administration published a formal notice that it intended to nullify that regulation.[12]

Assaults on medical privacy are also likely to increase. A proposal in President Obama's "economic stimulus plan" stipulated that every American's medical records be included in a government database, without any possibility of opting out. According to the Institute for Health Freedom, the goal is to have an electronic health record for each person in the United States by 2014—and all of these records would be accessible through a "nationwide health information technology infrastructure." Even if the promised safeguards against hacking into this database, and against the accidental dissemination of such information, were kept, the prospect of having one's health records in the hands of government officials is one many Americans find terrifying—especially in light of the growing sentiment that older or disabled persons sometimes "have a duty to die" in order to reduce the burden on younger, more productive members of society.

All the trends described above—to a large extent made possible by modern technology—are an example of how society now exercises a degree of control over individual citizens that earlier generations of Americans would have found incomprehensible, and utterly unacceptable.

NOTES

[1]*Dignatis Personae,* Sept. 8, 2008, no. 4.

²*Donum Vitae*, 1987, I, no. 1.

³A Reuters News Service report from July 2, 2003 stated that "Dr. Norbert Gleicher of the Foundation for Reproductive Medicine in Chicago and a colleague injected male cells into female embryos in research which they believe could lead to better treatments or cures for single gene disorders. But their work provoked revulsion when they presented it to the annual meeting of the European Society of Human Reproduction and Embryology (ESHRE)."

⁴Michael H. Brown, "Mythical 'Chimera' Was Associated with Disaster—Warning of Genetic Meddling," *SpiritDaily.com*, Jan. 9, 2006.

⁵Michael H. Brown, "For Your Discernment: 1990 'Prophecy' Foreseeing Events Followed by New One," *SpiritDaily.com*, Dec. 30, 2004.

⁶Joanna Swords, "The Diabolical Disorientation in the Secular World—'Health Care,'" The Fatima Center, 2008.

⁷*Ibid.*, op.cit. p. 2.

Ibid., op.cit. p. 3.

⁹Helpful websites in this regard include www.lawdepot.com and www.doyourproxy.org.

¹⁰"NRLC Registers Its Strong Opposition to Repeal of Pro-Life Conscience Protection Rules," *National Right to Life News* (April 2009), p. 10.

¹¹*Ibid.*, op.cit. p. 11.

¹²*Ibid.*, op.cit. p. 10.

Chapter 7

Growing Threats
to Freedom and Faith

In 2006 one expert stated, "The Internet will hold so much digital data that in five years it will be possible to find out [as a result of electronic surveillance] what an individual was doing at a specific time and place."[1] We are now living in a "surveillance society," in which government agencies will soon have the ability to keep track of our every move—a prospect reminiscent of George Orwell's frightening novel *1984*.

Electronic items relied upon every day by the average American are capable of being used against us. For instance, all newer cell phones carry a GPS device, allowing the phone's location (and presumably the owner's, as well) to be monitored by anyone with the proper knowledge and equipment. Also, the FBI has developed a means of remotely activating a cell phone's microphone, thus turning it into a listening device; thwarting this technique requires removing the phone's battery, not merely turning it off.[2]

Credit cards, shopper loyalty or store discount cards, and SMART cards are all capable of containing embedded microchips that allow a person's movements to be tracked by satellite.[3] (Indeed, SMART is said to stand for "Satellite Monitoring and Remote Tracking.) The technology for creating and implanting such microchips already exists. U. S. Passports issued over the last few years, for instance, specifically state: "This document contains sensitive electronics."

As a result of the 9-11 terrorist attacks, there's been a major push by government and law enforcement officials for something called Real ID, a system of uniform state drivers' licenses containing miniature identification chips compatible with biometric facial recognition technology. Real ID would interact with an enormous government database containing finger prints, iris scans, and other individual biometric data.[4] Widespread privacy concerns (including the outright refusal of some U. S. states to participate) may have made the movement toward Real ID politically untenable, but the government has an alternative in mind.

Enhanced drivers' licenses, or EDLs, are somewhat different from Real ID, but use the same technology, and are just as potentially dangerous. These documents would contain embedded chips, each with a unique identifying number, which could be accessed by a remote scanner—even while the license was inside a purse or wallet.[5] This technology could conceivably allow police officers or government agents to "take attendance" at an anti-government rally or other public event merely by walking through the crowd and electronically recording the identity of everyone present.

In 2005 an important book titled *Spychips* was published; it provides a thoroughly-researched description of the nature, use, and dangers of RFID chips (radio frequency identification). These tiny computer chips—some of them no larger than a grain of sand—allow items to be tracked from a distance. According to the authors, Katherine Albrecht and Liz McIntyre, RFID could be used

> to infringe upon civil liberties. The technology could give government officials the ability to electronically frisk citizens without their knowledge and set up invisible checkpoints on roads and in pedestrian zones to monitor their movements.[6]

The technology—and, just as importantly, the political climate—now exists for every new car to be manufactured with a built-in chip or transponder; this would not only allow the location of a car to be tracked in real time, but also allow authorities to send out an electronic signal disabling the vehicle (a natural progression from the current On-Star service, which can electronically unlock a car, or provide other assistance, for subscribing motorists). Disabling vehicles in such a manner would be quite legitimate in the pursuit and capture of fleeing criminals; however, the capability might easily be abused, with government agencies using it against innocent citizens guilty of nothing more than belonging to a politically incorrect group.[7]

Some major corporations and businesses have been big supporters of RFID because the technology allows them to control inventory and shipments through chipping delivery pallets and containers. That use of RFID is quite legitimate. However, some firms have been, or are, chipping *every single product* (including individual items of clothing). This use is quite different from the Universal Bar Code, in which the same code number is used for every item in that category (e.g., every bag of a certain brand of potato chips has the exact same code number printed on it).

Each individual RFID chip has a *unique* number, and by correlating items purchased with the shopper's discount card or credit card, not only can a "buying history" of that customer be created by the store, but the person's location can be recorded each time he or she passes within range of an RFID reader or scanner.[8]

Not only does the widespread use of RFID chips by government and business pose a threat to privacy and civil liberties; there are also health concerns associated with their use. According to *Spychips,*

RFID readers emit electromagnetic energy over wide swaths. Since global corporations hope to embed RFID readers into walls, floors, doorways, shelving—even in the refrigerators and medicine cabinets of our homes— we and are our children would be continually bombarded with energy emanating from these devices. Medical researchers have begun to raise questions about the long-term health effects of this type of chronic exposure to low levels of electromagnetic radiation.[9]

A company called Applied Digital Solutions has created what it calls a "VeriChip"—a glass encapsulated RFID tag that can be injected into human flesh.[10] *This technology is already being used.*

For instance, Mexico's attorney general had a chip implanted under the skin of his arm to allow him to be traced if he's kidnapped; the chip also allows him—and members of his staff, similarly chipped—access to a secure computerized crime database.[11] A beach club in Barcelona, Spain, allows its members to receive a chip via a syringe injection; an RFID reader can then recognize their identity and credit balance, and allow them entry into exclusive areas of the club.[12] A video surveillance company in Cincinnati now requires its employees to have the VeriChip implant in order to enter a secure data center.[13]

A particularly chilling scenario is described by an article in *Foreign Policy* (quoted in *Whistleblower* magazine):

Now imagine a world in which every newborn baby immediately has a little capsule implanted under his armpit. Inside are monitors, tiny amounts of hormones, a wireless transmitter and receiver. The device is powered by a battery like the one inside your watch. Surgical replacement of the capsule every five years is mandatory, strictly enforced, and, because it is very cheap, paid for the by state. . . . From birth, no moment in a person's life will go unmonitored. At each street corner, at the entrance to each home, perhaps even inside each room and under each bed, there will be a metal box, tamper-proof and solid enough to prevent burglary. Each box will contain a receiver and transmitter linked to a central computer. Every time a person passes near the box, an electronic report will go out. It will run somewhat as follows: "The level of the anger hormone carried in the bloodstream of No. KJ-090679883 is a little elevated. Inject 21 milligrams of the relevant antidote into his bloodstream to prevent him from turning violent."[14]

This trend not only has potentially severe repercussions in terms of civil liberties, but inevitably brings to mind the scriptural warning against taking the "mark of the beast," mentioned in the Book of Revelation (13:16ff; 14:9-10), and echoed in numerous contemporary private revelations. Also, the supposed security offered by the chip may be illusory; one expert has shown that it's actually quite easy to clone a VeriChip implanted in someone's arm, and then program a new chip with the same ID number.[15]

The potential abuse of technology can be directed not only against our bodies, but also against our minds. One example is HAARP (High-frequency Active Auroral Research Program), a military weapon which involves deliberately directing waves of electrical energy at a target. Engineers have experimented with this weapon by calibrating it to human brain wave frequencies for the purpose of widespread manipulation of thoughts and emotions.

A similar, little-known Pentagon technology known as the Silent Sound Spread Spectrum (SSSS) has been operational since the early 1990s; it allows for the implantation of specific thoughts and feelings in unsuspecting persons. During the Gulf War of 1991, American psychological operations experts used this technology to cause several hundred thousand Iraqi soldiers to surrender to Coalition forces without firing a shot.[16] This is yet another example of a technology offering a truly legitimate and even humane use, while also holding the capability of being horribly abused. (This, of course, is what one would expect if a sinister plan were being implemented: the beneficial aspects of a new technology would be emphasized and even demonstrated, while its potential dangers would be downplayed or denied.[17])

Yet another threat to our physical well-being comes from above: chemtrails—not contrails, which are naturally produced by larger airplanes, but *chemtrails*, in which aircraft deliberately discharge harmful chemicals behind them as they travel across the sky. There are Internet articles describing the process, including "A Mechanic's Statement," in which an anonymous airline employee describes how the government has been paying the airlines since at least 1998 to release special chemicals from commercial aircraft—as part of something called Project Cloverleaf. Supposedly, this is part of a conspiracy to reduce the world's population by at least 90% in the near future.

Conspiracy theories—especially those on the Internet—must always be taken with a grain of salt, but in this particular instance, several investigations by the mainstream media have uncovered disturbing information. In 2005 the Las Vegas Tribune reported that chemical trails over Las Vegas—which were appearing every weekend—contained the known carcinogen ethylene dibromide,[18] and a similar report was made by station KSLA News 12.[19] (This idea is supported by various private revelations. One visionary was allegedly told that "Our adversary is dropping germs, toxins, poisons, insect eggs, deadly larvae from chemtrails,"[20] and John Leary was supposedly told by Jesus that weapons grade bacteria are being spread over the population by chemtrails, resulting in chronic coughs and year-round flu-like symptoms, allergies, sinus problems, and other illnesses—for the purpose of spreading disease and destroying our immune systems.[21])

If only part of the information presented here is true—though, in fact, most of it has been documented and confirmed—then we are facing very serious threats to our liberty as Americans, and to our freedom to live as followers of Jesus Christ. Powerful governments almost always look to expand their power even further—and because religious believers are one of the few groups capable of mounting serious resistance to their plans (though not through the use of force), it's only natural that a movement toward authoritarianism or outright tyranny would involve plans to monitor and control committed Christians. Technology has become an indispensable tool in this process, and will likely play a key role in any coming restrictions on religious practice. Therefore, it's important for us to be aware of the spiritual threats posed by our technological society, and of some basic steps we can take to protect ourselves.

First of all, we must assume that all our telephone, fax, and e-mail communications are, or easily can be, monitored. (It's been known for years that the National Security Agency has the capability of recording and sorting through billions of phone calls, using computer programs to isolate keys words to determine which calls deserve closer examination.) Thus, we must be very careful about what we say—even in the privacy of our homes, for it's certainly possible that newer TVs and other electronic devices have hidden cameras or microphones.

Second, we might try to learn what we can about modern technology—specifically, about ways to protect ourselves from having it used against us. One example is a message to John Leary in which Jesus allegedly recommended wrapping SMART cards and other chipped items with aluminum foil to prevent the RFID chip from being read.[22]

Third, we must be careful that neither we nor our loved ones become overly-reliant upon technological devices; even if nothing secret or sinister is happening, spiritual harm can still come from devoting too much time and attention to television, the Internet, video games, and other such forms of entertainment.

Most importantly, we must make sure we have a good, loving, and trusting relationship with Jesus Christ, for He is the only One

Who can protect us from every danger—whether of a spiritual, physical, or technological nature. If our faith is strong and committed, we ultimately have nothing to fear; the Lord will guide us, protect us, and give us the strength and courage to face whatever may come.

As St. Paul writes in the Letter to the Romans, "I am convinced that neither death, nor life, nor angels, nor principalities, nor present things, nor *future things* [emphasis added], nor powers, nor height, nor depth, nor any other creation will be able to separate us from the love of God in Christ Jesus our Lord" (8:38-39). In St. John's Gospel, Jesus states, "I have overcome the world"(16:33)—and if we base our lives on this promise, nothing will conquer us or lead us astray.

NOTES

[1]Alexi Mostrous & Rob Evans, "Google and Surveillance," *The Guardian*, Nov. 3, 2006. This statement was made by Nigel Gilbert, a professor at the Royal Academy of Engineering. According to him, "The answer would come from a range of data, for instance video recordings or data-banks which store readings from electronic chips. Such chips embedded in people's clothing could track their movements. . . . Everything can be recorded forever."

[2]Ben Kage, "Big Brother is Listening," *NewsTarget*, Dec. 5, 2006.

[3]In a message of Jan. 3, 2006, visionary John Leary was allegedly told by Jesus, "My faithful, you will be monitored through your phones, by satellites, and by any smart cards in your possession. The tentacles of the evil one will be watching your every move."

[4]According to U. S. Representative Sam E. Rohrer, "The FBI is currently building a billion-dollar database to house an enormous amount of biometric data. While officially aimed at housing criminal and terrorist data, this database already retains finger prints, iris scans and other individual biometrics that the government collects on ordinary citizens." "Real ID: Connecting the Dots to an International ID," *The DeWeese Report*, Sept. 2008.

[5]Bob Unruh, "Washington State's Enhanced Driver's License," *WorldNet-Daily*, Feb. 28, 2009. According to this article, "The technology already has been implemented in Washington state, where it is promoted as an alternative to a passport for traveling to Canada. So far, the program is optional."

[6]Katherine Albrecht and Liz McIntyre, *Spychips: How Major Corporations*

and Government Plan to Track Your Every Move with RFID (Nelson Current, 2005), p. 5.

[7]Those who doubt such a possibility should consider something that happened in Missouri: An official document targeted supporters of certain libertarian or conservative politicians (Ron Paul, Chuck Baldwin, and Bob Barr), and "directed Missouri law enforcement to give special attention to those holding such political beliefs and consider them to be a security risk and potential terrorists. . . . anyone advocating limited government and objecting to the massive growth of the federal government [was] to be considered a security risk." From "The Battle in the States: Freedom vs. Protection, Tom DeWeese and Mark Lerner, *The DeWeese Report* (May 2009), p. 2. The same article also states that "The vendor who produces 95% of all driver's licenses has proposed a Real ID Solutions driver's license in which a citizen's 'political party affiliation' would be on the face of the driver's license" (p. 4).

Furthermore, the technological control of privately-owned automobiles by government agencies is closer than most people realize. "With a $16 million grant from the federal government, the University of Iowa is developing a Global Positioning Satellite system that can measure the mileage, apply a variable tax rate that will increase during rush hours and in high-traffic areas, calculate the total, charge a designated account card, *and shut down your automobile if unpaid when due* [emphasis added]. Some 2,700 automobiles in five states will be used in the test. . . . With such a system in every vehicle, the government can have virtual control over the population." From "Government Control Goes That Extra Mile," by Henry Lamb: *The DeWeese Report* (August 2009), p. 10.

[8]*Spychips* identifies Wal-Mart and Proctor & Gamble as two of the major driving forces behind this trend.

[9]Albrecht and McIntyre, op.cit. pp. 29-30.

[10]*Ibid.*, p. 179.

[11]Reported by Reuters on July 13, 2004.

[12]Sherrie Gossett, "Your Papers, Please," *WorldNetDaily.com,* April 14, 2004.

[13]Liz McIntyre I Katherine Albrecht, "Two U. S. Company Employees Injected with RFID Microchips," *NewsWithViews.com*, Feb. 10, 2006.

[14]Quoted in "Ominous Signs from the Globalists," Joseph Farah, *Whistleblower* (July 2009), p. 4. The same article quotes Juan Enriquex, managing director of Excel Medical Ventures, as saying, "We can now program life. . . . Several months ago, researchers at the J. Craig Venter Institute and Synthetic Genomics took a mycoplasma cell and inserted long strands of DNA into it, making the cell an entirely different species. In January 2008, the same team build and inserted the world's largest organic molecule into a cell—this is the equivalent of a computer software package to program cells. One year later they produced thousands of these programs in a single day." This means "one can write out a life code, manipulate a cell and execute a specified desired

function. It means we can convert cells into programmable manufacturing entities."

[15]"VeriChip RFID Implant Hacked!," *Caspian Newsletter,* Jan. 27, 2006.

[16]A. True Ott, PhD., "The Sound of Silence: The Antithesis of Freedom," *EducateYourself.org,* Dec. 15, 2008.

[17]There are those who feel something of the sort is happening with the government-mandated switchover to High Definition Digital TV. Why, with budget deficits higher than ever, is the federal government so eager to spend money helping consumers make this transition? Is it possible there's a plan to allow society's leaders to control and manipulate the thinking of mass numbers of citizens by such a means?

[18]Marcus K. Dalton, "Chemtrails Are Over Las Vegas," Tribune Media Group, Aug. 2005.

[19]"Chemtrails: Is U. S. Gov't Secretly Testing Americans 'Again'?, KSLA News 12, Shreveport, Louisiana, Nov. 9, 2007; updated Dec. 21, 2007.

[20]Alleged message from God the Father to Louise Tomkiel, April 12, 2007.

[21]Alleged message from Jesus to John Leary, Oct. 17, 2002.

[22]Alleged message from Jesus to John Leary, July 24, 2007.

Section C

Spiritual Assaults
and
Religious Counterfeits

Chapter 8

Young Americans in the Crosshairs

Warfare, deadly diseases, and grinding poverty touch the lives of millions of children and teenagers throughout the world. Thankfully, the vast majority of young Americans are spared these harsh realities; indeed, the average young person in the United States today has access to more material possessions, nutrition and health care, leisure and entertainment options, and educational and career possibilities than perhaps 99% of all the persons who've ever lived. These great blessings are accompanied, however, by severe challenges and temptations—so much so that it can be argued today's young people are growing up in the most spiritually and morally dangerous era in human history.

Consider the gauntlet American children and teens have to run today in order to reach adulthood in a reasonably healthy emotional and moral state. Assuming, first of all, that they survive their nine months in the womb (a right denied to over 50 million unborn children since 1973), young people may be victims of poverty (something still not eliminated in the richest society in history), childhood diseases, or single-parent homes (a severe disadvantage, despite the efforts of even the most loving and conscientious single-parents). Young Americans may find easily themselves trapped in substandard government schools, and even in the better public schools, they're often subject to indoctrination (or brainwashing) in the latest social ideologies and politically correct fads; at the same time, they're subject to intense peer pressure and massive cultural propaganda—and these influences tend to undermine the credibility and authority of parents and the Church and denigrate those traditional moral values necessary for true and lasting happiness, while promoting rebellion, spiritual anarchy, and self-destructive behavior in the form of drug and alcohol abuse, sexual immorality, and sometimes even violence.

All these dangers might be included in any standard sociological analysis of American culture today—but from a spiritual or religious perspective, there are additional, even greater hazards. Scripture and Church teaching assert that, knowingly or unknowingly, all human beings are constantly involved in spiritual warfare; Satan and his evil spirits seek the eternal damnation of every person now alive on earth, young and old alike. At one time Catholic children and teens were taught this sobering truth, and instructed in the use of the Church's spiritual weapons given by Christ to help them emerge triumphant from their lifelong spiritual combat. In the turmoil which followed the Second Vatican Council, however, several decades of vacuous religious "education" have left millions of American Catholics standing on a very shaky spiritual and moral foundation—while also leaving these adult Catholics poorly equipped to offer spiritual guidance and protection to their own children.

Jesus taught that children and young people are especially precious to their Father in Heaven (cf. Mt. 18:1-5); therefore, it's reasonable to assume the devil takes great efforts to lead the young into sin, despair, self-destruction, and damnation—and a look at American society provides plenty of evidence to support this view. Never before have the young been under such intense attack—and rarely have so many of them, through no fault of their own, been so ill-equipped to resist—and this has grave implications for society as a whole. As one commentator notes,

> The root of moral decay in a society is rebellion. It has become acceptable among the youth of today at a very

formative and vulnerable point in their lives. Many of those affected previously are now the parents and grandparents of today who in their lifetime have witnessed the fastest, most consistent decline of morality in the history of the planet.[1]

Some of the weapons the adversary uses against our young people are obvious, including temptations in the areas of rebellion, rejection of parental and religious authority, peer pressure, cliques, an obsession with one's social status (often with corresponding efforts to undermine or destroy the status of others), drug and alcohol abuse, greed and materialism, and sexual immorality. However, the devil has many other spiritual snares for unsuspecting youths—some very blatant, but others much more carefully disguised (and, for that reason, all the more potentially dangerous).

Today most children's TV programs, animated movies, videos, and cartoons are awash in humanism and New Age symbolism.[2] For instance, one very popular and widespread phenomenon among children is the Pokemon craze. This simulation game, first released in 1995 by Nintendo, has

an undeniable emphasis on teaching children to fight, kill, poison, and to use psychic and occultic powers to accomplish their goals. Additionally, the world of Pokemon is teaching children that evolution, supernatural powers, and violence are all perfectly acceptable concepts.[3]

Pokemon (short for *pocket monsters*) trains impressionable children in basic New Age ideas,[4] and may even involve a degree of physical danger. (For instance, a series of mass seizures occurred in Japan while children were viewing a Pokemon television program on December 16, 1997; this event resulted in *seven hundred* hospitalizations.)

An even greater phenomenon is the worldwide popularity of the *Harry Potter* books and movies, which have garnered hundreds of millions of fans—not only among children, but among teens and adults as well. Most people view the stories as harmless fantasy, and there are Catholic commentators who consider them religiously acceptable and even useful tools for family discussions;[5] however, many other observers have a far less favorable view. Fr.

Gabriele Amorth, chief exorcist of the Vatican, was quoted as saying, "You start off with Harry Potter, who comes across as a likeable wizard, but you end up with the devil. There is no doubt that the signature of the Prince of Darkness is clearly within these books."[6] Even more significant are the words of Cardinal Josef Ratzinger (the future Pope Benedict XVI), who in 2003 wrote to Gabriele Kuby, Germany's best known critic of Harry Potter, "It is good that you enlighten people about Harry Potter, because those are subtle seductions, which act unnoticed and by this deeply distort Christianity in the soul, before it can grow properly."[7]

What are the religious and spiritual objections to these wildly popular books and movies? One expert writes,

There is, of course, plenty of courage and love in the Harry Potter series, but it is this very mixing of truth and untruth which makes it so deceptive. Courage and love can be found in all peoples, even those involved in the worst forms of paganism. The presence of such virtues does not automatically justify an error-filled work of fiction. In Potter-world the characters are engaged in activities which in real life corrupt us, weaken the will, darken the mind, and pull the practitioner down into spiritual bondage.

Rowling's characters go deeper and deeper into that world without displaying any negative side effects, only an increase in "character." This is a lie. Moreover, it is *the* Satanic lie which deceived us in Eden.[8]

The concepts of good and evil certainly exist in the Harry Potter series, but they aren't clearly defined—and even the "good" characters participate in such Scripturally-forbidden activities as sorcery, astrology, casting spells, and communicating with the dead (cf. Dt. 18:10-14).[9] Also, while author J. K. Rowling claims that the spells contained in the books are made up, she acknowledged, "I have met people who assure me, very seriously, that they are trying to do them"[10] (and she also admitted to receiving more than a few letters from young readers begging, in all seriousness, to be admitted as students to Hogwarts—the fictional school of magic in the books and movies).

Not everyone agrees with Rowling's claims on the harmlessness of the spells described in her books. Clare McGrath Merkle, a former New Age "healer" and advanced yoga practitioner who has since returned to the Catholic faith, writes:

Many of the delightfully described magical arts in the Harry Potter series were pretty standard fare in training courses I mastered to some degree or another, including telepathy, divination, energy-work, necromancy, geomancy and time-travel, to name but a few. . . . A close reading of one of the books in the series, *Harry Potter and the Prisoner of Azkaban* . . . by the eyes of a former occultist like myself, reveals her [Rowling's] more than cursory familiarity with the occult.[11]

As another author warns,

Witchcraft and sorcery permeate Rowling's books, and parents would do well to attempt the impossible: steer kids clear of Hogwarts School of Witchcraft and Wizardry. At the very least, children determined to explore Harry Potter's realm should be grounded in a flame-retardant faith, that enables them to ride the lightning and still walk away unscathed.[12]

Because parents are the first and most important educators of their children in the ways of faith (cf. *Catechism*, par. 2225-2226), they should, at the very least, discuss with them the moral choices and situations facing the characters in the Harry Potter stories ("Was this the right thing for Harry to do? How would God want someone facing those circumstances to respond?"); they would also do well to supplement (and perhaps eventually replace) Rowling's books with classic Christian literature, such as C. S. Lewis' *The Chronicles of Narnia* and J. R. R. Tolkien's *The Lord of the Rings* trilogy.

The popularity of Harry and his friends has led to an increased interest in witchcraft and paganism among young people,[13] though involvement in Wicca was already at an all-time high by the end of the 20th century. Wicca, which means bending nature to one's own purposes,[14] is a revival of ancient witchcraft and pagan traditions. Young women may be especially attracted to it because of its emphasis on a feminine deity ("the Goddess," accompanied by her consort, "the horned God"). While some Wiccans meet in covens or circles, others cast spells or practice Wiccan rituals alone.[15]

Wiccans insist they are not Satanists (and in fact, Wiccans and Satanists often resent and disparage each other[16]); while they acknowledge the reality of "black magic," they claim to practice only "white," or good magic, involving earth rituals, an appreciation of nature, and the casting of beneficial spells. However, from a Christian perspective, this claim is gravely mistaken: there are only two possible sources of spiritual power, and anything not clearly of God (as judged by the authority of Scripture and the Church) can only come from the devil.

It is very easy for young people today, whether out of simple curiosity or an actual rebellion against parental authority and organized religion, to become involved in witchcraft and the occult:

> Never before has destructive occultism been hawked so crassly directly to teenagers through metal music, movies and videos, and even comic books and magazines. Until the last three decades, the primary source of information on occult subjects was word of mouth, secondarily through books. A typical teenager's closest brush with the occult was playing with an Ouija board or giggling through a mock séance at a slumber party. Today's teenagers are confronted on every side with the commercialized occult.[17]

The Internet has made witchcraft more accessible than ever, with web sites allowing teens to take online classes in the occult, attend the "Church and School of Wicca," or have spells cast on their behalf.[18] Naturally, parents need to be alert for warning signs, including their teen's extreme alienation from family members, drug and alcohol use, an excessive need to be in control, a sense of powerlessness, or an attraction to the bizarre and mysterious.[19] Other possible indications might be difficulty relating to peers, an inability to fit in with the structures of school and society, violent aggression, cruelty to animals, a sudden alienation from friends and routine activities, a drastic drop in grades, and an obsessive interest in heavy metal music.[20]

One expert suggests that parents worried over their teen's possible involvement in the occult should avoid panic or overreaction (as the person's interest may be only a passing fad); instead, they should observe behavior and gather evidence before confronting their child, and ask questions and listen rather than accuse; if the situation seems serious, professional help should be obtained.[21]

Many young people first become exposed to the occult through role-playing games such as Dungeons & Dragons; indeed, Anton LaVey, the founder of the Church of Satan in southern California, has stated that such games are the best way to indoctrinate youth into the occult.[22] Many critics have pointed out the grave dangers associated with such games; young people are exposed to deceptive spiritual ideas, and have sometimes been influenced to act in violent ways, including crime, rape, sexual abuse, suicide, and even murder.[23] Moreover, the game's instructions make "no attempt to camouflage the demonic nature of the game's extremely occultic components."[24]

A still more pervasive threat to young people today is the widespread popularity of rock, punk, and heavy metal music (and their various offshoots). Music's power to influence human emotions has long been recognized; the ancient philosopher Plato observed, "When modes of music change, the fundamental laws of the state change with them," and his contemporary Aristotle believed that because it's so powerful, all music for the young should be controlled or restricted by the state. Early in the 20th century the Communist revolutionary Vladimir Lenin claimed, "One quick way to destroy a society is through its music," and the late rock musician Jimmy Hendrix insisted, "Music is a spiritual thing of its own. You can hypnotize people with music, and when you get people at the weakest point, you can preach into the subconscious what you want to say."[25]

The average teen listens to over ten thousand hours of music between seventh and twelfth grade (more than twice as much time as spent in the classroom during the high school years), and, as one author notes, "anything we are exposed to this much has got to have an influence on us."[26] Some rock or heavy metal music, though incomprehensible and unattractive to parents, is morally unobjectionable, and there are even Christian heavy metal bands; much of the genre, however, is deliberately and explicitly Satanist, while often promoting self-destructive behavior:

The lyrics of many songs, such as *Highway to Hell,*
Die Young—Die Pretty, Destroy Yourself, and *The*
Suicide Solution, are explicit invitations to commit

suicide, to give oneself over to the service of Satan. Small wonder, then, that among people listening to such music the thought of suicide becomes an obsession.[27]

One expert, the Italian psychiatrist Dr. Simone Morabito, notes,

For us psychiatrists [Satanic rock music] is a like a slow-acting, highly effective poison. Our medical journals inform us that in recent years 5000 young people in the USA have taken their lives. I am convinced that one of the chief causes of these suicides is satanic rock music that promotes the taking of one's life.[28]

In addition to explicitly satanic and self-destructive messages found in the lyrics of some songs, heavy metal music (especially at concerts and in discos) is harmful because of the extreme volume (110 decibels or more), especially when combined with stroboscopic lights and the use of alcohol or narcotics; such excessive stimulation can cause irreversible damage to the brain;[29] moreover, the increase of adrenaline in the bloodstream can make the music physically addictive.[30] According to one researcher, music "consecrated" to the devil has a powerful rhythm (which mimics the sexual act), is at least seven decibels higher than the tolerance of our nervous system (ultimately inducing a type of depression, rebellion, and aggressiveness), and uses subliminal signals (transmitted at a pitch too high for human hearing, but capable of being picked up by our subconscious minds).[31]

Certain hard rock groups have acted in bizarre and disturbing ways; for instance, the band Hell on Earth had planned to feature an on-stage suicide of a terminally ill person (though this was prevented by authorities), and is known for such repulsive stage acts as grinding up live rats in a blender.[32] King Diamond of the Satanist band Mercyful Fate used a microphone stand made of human leg bones,[33] and one group, Red Hot Chili Peppers, publicly thanked Satan for their success at the MTV awards.[34]

According to a former rock musician named Eric Barger, Listening to rock music never sent anyone to Hell. No, it simply teaches people how to get there, destroys

God's desire for one's life, produces idolatry and
conditions those who listen with satanic ideals.
Certainly, not every song on rock and country radio is
evil. . . . It's every third, fifth, eighth, fifteenth or
twentieth song that teaches the adversary's goals
explicitly. Many of the other songs may not be as
blatant, but they still fall far short of the standard which
God is pleased with. And that's really the key isn't it?
Who and what are we identifying with? What are we
advocating?[35]

Much more could be written about the spiritual threats facing
our youth today. Having lost his own original spiritual purity and
beauty, Satan hates innocence, and he takes a special delight in
ensnaring and destroying the souls of young people. His weapons
are many, varied, and exceedingly dangerous—and, in today's increasingly post-Christian society, more effective than ever. Parents
concerned over the spiritual well-being of their children may often
feel overwhelmed, but the Lord expects them, rather than giving
up in despair or merely hoping for the best, to take a proactive
stance, using the spiritual weapons He has provided.

Living out the grace of one's baptism (and teaching children to
do the same), active involvement in a parish, carefully arranging
for the religious education of one's children, family prayer, shared
reading of Scripture and other spiritual books, discussions on moral
issues, encouraging involvement in parish and community activities for young people, fellowship with other families sharing similar
values and worldviews, giving an example of moral integrity and
commitment, and maintaining an attitude of acceptance and an
openness to dialogue, are all ways of forming godly children and
young people, and equipping them for spiritual combat. Fulfilling such parental duties has become perhaps more important than
ever before in history, and God's blessings and peace will surely
be given to those mothers and fathers who attempt to do so in a
spirit of prayerful humility and trust.

NOTES

[1]Eric Barger, *From Rock to Rock: The Music of Darkness Exposed* (Huntington House, 1990), p. 14.

[2]Phil Arms, *Pokemon & Harry Potter: A Fatal Attraction* (Heathstone Publishing, 2000), pp. 9-10.

[3]*Ibid.*, p. 30.

[4]Arms writes, "All of the Pokemon productions share the same goal to train children how to become the number one Pokemon Master in the world. This term 'master' is a non-subtle, in-your-face, giveaway to the fundamental nature of Pokemon. Becoming a 'master' is part of the vocabulary and goal orientation of Zen Buddhism, the New Age meditative arts, and other Eastern religions" (p. 25).

[5]See, for instance, Nancy Carpentier Brown's *The Mystery of Harry Potter—A Catholic Family Guide* (Our Sunday Visitor Publishing, 2007).

[6]John-Henry Westen, "Vatican's Chief Exorcist Repeats Condemnation of Harry Potter Novels," *LifeSiteNews.com,* March 2, 2006. The article also states, "In a 2002 interview with the Italian ANSA news agency, Rev. Amorth said 'Behind Harry Potter hides the signature of the king of the darkness, the devil.' The exorcist, with his decades of experience in directly combating evil, explained that J. K. Rowling's books contain innumerable positive references to magic, 'the satanic art.' He noted that the books attempt to make a false distinction between black and white magic, when in fact, the distinction 'does not exist, because magic is always a turn to the devil.'"

[7]*Ibid.*

[8]Michael D. O'Brien, "Harry Potter and the Paganization of Children's Culture," *The Catholic World Report* (April 2001), p. 59.

[9]Kristin Sparks, "Should Your Children Read Harry Potter?," *HLI Reports* (December 2000), p. 7.

[10]*Ibid.*

[11]Clare McGrath Merkle, "Harry Potter and the Lost Generations."www.crossveil.org/potter.html.

[12]Ellen Makkai, "Harry the Wiz is the Wrong Biz," *WorldNetDaily.com,* Nov. 26, 2001.

[13]Sparks, op.cit. p. 7. The media officer of the Pagan Federation in England was quoted as saying, "In response to the increased inquiries coming from youngsters we established a young officer . . . to answer these queries and to allow someone to offer advice and information. It is quite probably linked to things like Harry Potter, Sabrina the Teenage Witch and Buffy the Vampire Slayer. Every time an article on witchcraft or paganism appears, we had a

huge surge in calls, mostly from young girls."

[14]Catherine Edwards, "Wicca Casts Spell on Teen-Age Girls," *Insight*, Oct. 25, 1999.

[15]Catherine Edwards, "Wicca Infiltrates the Churches," *Insight*, Dec. 6, 1999.

[16]Marcia Montenegro, *Spellbound: The Paranormal Seduction of Today's Kids* (Life Journey, 2006), p. 127.

[17]Bob & Gretchen Passantino, *When the Devil Dares Your Kids* (Servant Books, 1991), p. 107.

[18]Steve Russo, *Protecting Your Teen from Today's Witchcraft* (Bethany House, 2005), p. 52.

[19]Passantino, op.cit. pp. 17ff.

[20]Rev. Thomas Knoblach, "Satanism: The Problem and the Response," *Homiletic & Pastoral Review* (Oct. 1991).

[21]*Ibid.* Helpful information, and assistance or referrals, can be obtained-from such sites as www.parenthelpcenter.org (1-800-688-8706), www.catholic-parents.org., and www.parentproject.com. Recommended books include *Spellbound: The Paranormal Seduction of Today's Kids,* by Marcia Montenegro (Life Journey, 2006); *Protecting Your Teen From Today's Witchcraft,* by Steve Russo (Bethany House, 2005); and *Overcoming the Power of the Occult,* by Terry Ann Modica (Faith Publishing Company, 1996).

[22]Arms, op.cit. p. 40.

[23]Arms, op.cit., p. 70. In his book *The Satan Hunter* (Daring Books, 1988), Thomas W. Wedge quotes a psychiatrist named Dr. Thomas Radecki as saying, "The evidence in these cases is really quite impressive. There is no doubt in my mind that the game Dungeons & Dragons is causing young men to kill themselves and others. . . . Based on player interviews and game materials, it is clear to me that this game is desensitizing players to violence, and, also, causing an increased tendency to violent behavior" (p. 104).

[24]Arms, op.cit. p. 68.

[25]Pat Pulling, *The Devil's Web—Who Is Stalking Your Children for Satan?* (Huntington House, 1989), p. 103. In his article "The Moral Power of Music," (*Homiletic & Pastoral Review,* April 2002), Fr. Basil Nortz quotes the 6th century philosopher Boethius as warning, "Music can both establish and destroy morality. For no path is more open to the soul for the formation thereof than through the ears." He also quotes the 19th century American author Henry David Thoreau: "Music can be intoxicating. Such apparently slight causes destroyed Greece and Rome, and will destroy England and America" (p. 17).

[26]Russo, op.cit. p. 21.

[27]Fr. Mieczyslaw Piotrowski S. Chr,, "Satan in Music?," *Love One Another* (no. 12), p. 39.

[28]*Ibid.*

[29]*Ibid.*, pp. 39-40.

[30]Nortz, p. 21 (cf. #25 above).

[31]Michael H. Brown, "Music from Sixties Had Direct Links with Elements that Were Often Dark, Devilish," *SpiritDaily.com,* June 19, 2006.

[32]Russo, p. 22.

[33]Wedge, p. 88 (cf. #23 above).

[34]Brown, op.cit. It's instructive to note that many of the musicians who, in effect, "sold their souls" to the devil by promoting Satanism in their music, came to an unhappy end. Mr. Brown refers to Robert Johnson, the king of the delta blues, who supposedly made a pact with the evil one; just before he died he was supposedly "barking and howling like a dog." Kurt Kobain, who sang the words "We will get stoned and worship Satan," committed suicide. John Lennon, who was murdered by a man who "heard voices" urging his shooting, had admitted that he was more of a channeler of spirits than a musician, and that he and Paul McCartney both felt at times that they were in communication with spirits. The average American lives to age 78; the average lifespan of rock, punk, and heavy-metal stars is only 37.

[35]Barger, op.cit. p. iv.

Chapter 9

The New Age Movement

Early in 2009, Trinity College of Hartford, Connecticut released the results of its third American Religious Identification Survey, which was conducted in 2008. Compared to the first survey, taken in 1990, the number of Catholics in the United States grew by just over 11 million, but other changes might be considered less favorable to traditional religion.

The percentage of Americans calling themselves Christian declined from 86% in 1990 to 76% in 2008, while the number of atheists increased to 1.6 million (nearly doubling from 2001, the year of the second survey). The number of persons claiming to believe in God, but not identifying themselves with any particular religion, has increased dramatically, as have the number of Wiccans, self-described pagans, and other persons with vague religious ideas.[1]

Given the state of American society today, these figures are no surprise: growing numbers of people claim to be "spiritual" but not "religious;" they are looking for some deeper meaning in life, something promising a sense of purpose, fellowship, and personal fulfillment—but without having to make any real sacrifices or commitment. This, of course, is a false understanding of what religion and spirituality are supposed to be, and it ignores the clear warning of Scripture. 2 Tim. 4:3-4 says, "For the time will come when people will not tolerate sound doctrine but, following their own desires and insatiable curiosity, will accumulate teachers and will stop listening to the truth, and will be diverted to myths." This description certainly seems to apply to the New Age Movement.

The New Age Movement (NAM) is a loosely-structured, worldwide network of thousands of cooperating organizations, and millions of individuals, including government officials, scientists, environmentalists, health care workers, athletes, celebrities, and members of some (though not all) religious cults. [2]New Agers borrow ideas and practices from many different sources, including meditation techniques from Hinduism, Zen, and Native American religion; humanistic psychology; occult rituals; and modern science and technology.[3] The underlying idea is that our human nature is capable of continually transforming and transcending itself—but that Western civilization (specifically, Christianity) has imposed artificial and unnecessary limitations on this process.

According to New Agers, humanity must break free of this spiritual bondage by achieving a new awareness of its potential—indeed, of its own divinity. When enough people have reached this breakthrough point, all humanity will come to a "god consciousness," completing the evolutionary process.[4] When this occurs, humanity will leave behind the current 2000 year period dominated by the sign of Pisces (the fish, symbolizing Christianity), and move into the glorious new age of Aquarius, a time of peace and enlightenment.[5]

On a more personal scale, New Age adherents do their part to achieve synergy, or maximum spiritual union and power, by moving from one New Age fad to another, seeking the one that will awaken the "divine energy" within them—with the knowledge that if they're unsuccessful in this life, reincarnation will give them as many opportunities as necessary to complete this process.[6]

The NAM does not believe in a personal God—and certainly not the God of Christianity; rather, it claims, divinity is to be found within us. There have also been, however, certain enlightened individuals throughout history whose role is to help the rest of us find our way; these "Ascended Masters," as they're sometimes called, supposedly include Gandhi, Mohammed, Buddha, Krishna, and even Jesus. (The NAM rejects the idea of Jesus Christ as Savior of the world, but is careful not to attack Him directly; instead, it tries to diminish His influence by making Him merely one of a series of important religious figures.) According to New Agers, Jesus is not "the" Christ, or Savior; that role is reserved for the coming World Teacher known as Maitreya, who will be god incarnate.[7] (This idea will be explored in more depth in the next chapter.)

New Age dogma is expressed by eight major themes: mystery teachings, occultism and Eastern mysticism, psychology or an emphasis on the powers of the mind, the importance of science and technology in humanity's search for meaning and identity, evolution, hedonism, pantheism (the belief that all creation is divine), and leadership by spiritually superior beings. [8]Techniques used by various New Agers include visualization and guided imagery (a potentially powerful and dangerous method of getting in touch with the spirit world),[9] transcendental meditation, music and color therapy, incense, sexual ritual, drug ingestion, yoga,[10] automatic writing, and the channeling of spirits by mediums,[11] along with psychotherapy, biofeedback, hypnosis, and holistic medicine. (A few of these techniques may be legitimate in and of themselves, but it's easy for them to be misused.) Popular New Age programs include Silva Mind Control (whose founder, Jose Silva, claims that his meditation techniques are similar to those taught by Jesus to His disciples, even though there is no scriptural support for this idea[12]), and the so-called "Course in Miracles," which uses Christian terminology but is incompatible with Christianity—for it claims that God did not create the world, that Jesus is not the only Son of God, and that He did not die for our sins.[13]

New Age adherents claim they're merely incorporating the "best" of Eastern mysticism with Western science and knowledge; what many of them don't realize, or aren't told, is that much of this mysticism is actually nothing more than Hinduism.[14] For instance, New Agers often use a "mantra," or a mystical word repeated over and over, to help them enter into a trance-like state. The founder of Transcendental Meditation, Maharishi Mahesh Yogi, claimed that each person's mantra was unique (and should never be shared with anyone else). Other sources revealed, however, that the mantra was invariably the name of a Hindu god.[15]

Certain elements of the NAM also have an occultic dimension, claiming that witchcraft can be used for either white or black magic—but, as pointed out in the previous chapter, Christianity claims that all spiritual powers not originating in Christ are of Satan. Practitioners of "white" magic—which is supposedly natural and benign—claim to be serving friendly spiritual powers, such as Kali, Lilith, Pan, and Shiva; however, *The Satanic Bible*, by Anton Szandor LaVey, includes these names in a list of "infernal names," or synonyms for Satan.[16]

The NAM does have several good points, including a respect for creation and a desire to protect it, an emphasis on proper care of the body, and the promotion of world peace. It's important to avoid the assumption that all New Age practices and adherents are automatically opposed to Christianity.[17] However, it cannot be denied that some major New Age spokespersons have demonstrated unmistakable hostility toward the Church. Anti-Catholicism pervades the writings of the late Alice Bailey, whom many New Agers revere as a patroness and leading light of the Movement. For instance, her 1957 book *The Externalization of the Hierarchy* states that nuclear weapons must be taken away from individual countries, but preserved for use by the United Nations—as a threat to forestall any aggressive action by a nation, political group, or powerful religious organization such as *the Church of Rome*.[18]

The writings of David Spangler, an important New Age author, state that those of us who refuse to accept the coming Universal Teacher (*"the* Christ") will be sent to "another dimension other than physical incarnation," where we'll supposedly be happier—and unable to interfere with the Movement's plans.[19] The NAM has also been accused of being profoundly anti-Semitic, and some of its authors insist that, in the coming New Age, religious freedom and the separation between church and state will come to an end.[20]

Because of its widespread popularity, and its influence with certain government agencies[21] and big business,[22] the NAM has become very powerful—and this can represent a grave spiritual danger to unwary Christians. One Christian author notes that because the New Age seeks to replace Judaism and Christianity with its own One World religion, the Movement is attempting to discredit, infiltrate, and deceive the leaders and members of synagogues and churches.[23] There is in fact a New Age cult specializing in converting Catholics to the Movement: something called the "Church Universal and Triumphant."[24] This deceptively-named group combines a conservative political agenda and traditional family values with a deliberately distorted use of Catholic concepts and terminology. In particular, CUT attracts Catholics through supposedly reverencing the Virgin Mary, who is labeled an "Ascended Master," like her Son, Jesus; also, CUT's variation of the Sign of the Cross is clearly heretical: "In the Name of the Father, the Mother, the Son, and the Holy Spirit."[25]

In speaking of Hinduism and Buddhism, the Vatican II document *Declaration on the Relation of the Church to Non-Christian Religions* states, "The Catholic Church rejects nothing of what is true and holy in these religions. . . . Yet she proclaims and is in duty bound to proclaim without fail, Christ who is the way, the truth, and the life (John 1:6)" (n. 2). This means that Catholics are not free "to engage in the religious practices and rituals of these religions [which underlie much of the NAM], nor adopt aspects of their religious beliefs and philosophies into their own worldview."[26]

Because the beliefs of Catholicism and the NAM are fundamentally irreconcilable,[27] Catholics cannot formally or directly involve themselves in the Movement; moreover, they must be careful not to engage in any apparently beneficial or benign spiritual practices that might in fact lead them astray. (An example would be deliberately seeking mystical experiences through such New Age techniques as yoga, visualization, hypnotism, the use of mantras and spirit guides, and the channeling of spirits—for authentic Christian mysticism is never self-induced, but always results from the free action of the Holy Spirit.[28])

The NAM, in its belief in reincarnation (an idea explicitly rejected by the Bible—Heb. 9:27), its denial of a personal God and the reality of divine judgment, its vulnerability to manipulation by evil spirits, and its lack of humility (in proudly boasting we are all divine), is spiritually misleading and dangerous—and thus one more powerful tool for Satan in his ongoing assault on the Church.

NOTES

[1]Chaz Muth, "Percentage of Catholics Down, But Church Still Largest U. S. Denomination," *Catholic News Service*, March 20, 2009.

[2]Constance Cumbey, *The Hidden Dangers of the Rainbow* (Huntington House, 1983), p. 54.

[3]Mitch Pacwa, S. J., *Catholics and the New Age* (Servant Publications, 1992), p. 14.

⁴Johnette S. Benkovic, *The New Age Counterfeit* (Queenship Publishing, 1993), p. 2.

⁵Pacwa, op.cit. p. 16. In this regard, it's interesting to read some of the lyrics of the song "Aquarius" (from the mid-1960s rock musical "Hair"): "When the moon is in the seventh house, and Jupiter aligns with Mars, then peace will guide the planets, and love will steer the stars. This is the dawning of the age of Aquarius, the age of Aquarius. . . . Harmony and understanding, sympathy and trust abounding; no more falsehoods or derisions, golden living dreams of visions, mystic crystal revelation, and the mind's true liberation," etc.

⁶*Ibid.*

⁷Texe Marrs, *Dark Secrets of the New Age* (Crossway Books, 1987), p. 59.

⁸*Ibid.*, pp. 189-190.

⁹Dave Hunt & T. A. McMahon, *The Seduction of Christianity* (Harvest House Publishers, 1985), p. 123.

¹⁰F. LaGard Smith, "New Age Prayer," *New Covenant* (June 1989), p. 10. Smith writes, "The purpose of yoga is to achieve altered consciousness. Its very name *yoga* is derived from the Sanskrit term for 'yoke' or 'union.' Altered consciousness is supposed to lead to a oneness with Brahman, the god-force of Hinduism. Thus the ultimate goal of yoga is achieving oneness with deity."

¹¹Marrs, op.cit. p. 106.

¹²*Ibid.*, pp. 112-113.

¹³Russell Chandler, *Understanding the New Age* (Word Publishing, 1988), pp. 212-213.

¹⁴Marrs, op.cit. pp. 46-47.

¹⁵*Ibid.*, p. 114.

¹⁶Cumbey, op.cit. p. 136.

¹⁷Chandler, op.cit. pp. 222-223.

¹⁸Alice A. Bailey, *The Externalization of the Hierarchy* (Lucis Publishing Company, 1957), p. 548. According to Texe Marrs (in *New Age Cults & Religions*), the Lucis Publishing Company—the source of Bailey's book—is a subsidiary of the Lucis Trust. This organization, when founded by Alice Bailey, was originally known as Lucifer Publishing (p. 238). Presumably the original name was considered too revealing, and so it was changed in 1922.

¹⁹Cumbey, op.cit. p. 69.

²⁰*Ibid.*

²¹*Ibid.*, pp. 129-130. Mrs. Cumbey notes, "According to Marilyn Ferguson and other New Age writers, the government has long since been infiltrated by active New Age conspirators. In her public lectures, Ms. Ferguson relates that she was even invited to be the keynote speaker at the 1982 Department of

Defense annual dinner. Her book [*The Aquarian Conspiracy*] freely relates that there are conspirators at the Cabinet level, the White House staff, congressmen—at every level of government. According to her book, The National Institute of Mental Health (NIMH), the Department of Health, Education, and Welfare, and Department of Defense—not to mention the corruption of the grant writing process of the United States government to fund these quasi-religious/openly 'religious' programs of the New Age Movement—include Zen, Transcendental Meditation, and other psycho-technologies of every shade and description in their programs."

[22]Marrs, p. 31. For instance, "on September 28, 1986 *The New York Times* reported that during the previous July 'representatives of some of the nation's largest corporations, including IBM, AT & T, and General Motors, met in New Mexico to discuss how metaphysics, the occult, and Hindu mysticism might help executives compete in the world marketplace.' Furthermore, 'at Stanford University's renowned Graduate School of Business, a seminar called 'Creativity in Business' includes such topics as chanting, meditation, the use of tarot cards, and the 'New Age Capitalist.' Meanwhile, a recent survey of five hundred corporate presidents and company owners revealed that half had sponsored some type of New Age 'consciousness raising technique' for their employees."

[23]*Ibid.*, p. 206.

[24]Pacwa, op.cit. p. 164.

[25]*Ibid.*, p. 167.

[26]Benkovic, op.cit. pp. 16-17.

[27]This point becomes self-evident after a study of the following Scripture passages: Deut. 18:10-11; Is. 55:8; Mt. 7:13-16; Mt. 12:36-37; Mk. 9:42; Jn. 8:31-32; Rm. 12:2; 1 Cor. 1:18-19; 1 Cor. 2:1-2,5; 1 Cor. 2:11-14; 2 Cor. 11:14-15; 1 Tim. 4:1-2; 2 Tim. 4:3-4; Col. 2:8; 1 Jn. 2:22; 1 Jn. 5:19; 1 Pt. 5:8; and 2 Pt. 2:1-2.

Also, the *Catechism of the Catholic Church* makes it unmistakably clear that New Age beliefs and practices are incompatible with divine revelation and Catholic teaching; see par. 2108, 2115, 2116, and 2117.

[28]Benkovic, op.cit. p. 37.

Chapter 10

Manifestation—or Manipulation?

On December 12, 2008, a New Age organization called *Share International* put out a news release (on the Dow Jones & Company's Market Watch website, no less) stating that a large, bright star would appear in the sky in the very near future—a so-called "Christmas Miracle." This star would supposedly be visible, day and night, throughout the world—and would foretell the imminent and, for New Agers, long-desired arrival of the World Teacher known as the Lord Maitreya, along with his colleagues, the "Masters of Wisdom."

According to the news release, "Awaited by all faiths under different names, Maitreya is the Christ to Christians, the Imam Mahdi to Muslims, Krishna to Hindus, the Messiah to Jews, and Maitreya Buddha to Buddhists. He is the World Teacher for all, religious or not, an educator in the broadest sense."[1]

In 1982, a New Age author named Benjamin Creme, Maitreya's self-appointed publicist, announced that the World Teacher was alive but living in private, preparing for his mission, and in 1988 Maitreya supposedly appeared in a miraculous manner to some 6000 people in Kenya. Since then, however, he's been waiting for the proper time to begin his mission of enlightening humanity. According to the December 12, 2008 press release, once the star appears in the sky, Maitreya will be interviewed one week later on a major U. S. television program—and this would mark the imminent arrival of the New Age. (Needless to say, the "Christmas Miracle" star didn't appear on schedule—presumably causing great disappointment to Maitreya and his followers.)

From a Christian perspective, the obvious reaction to this cosmic publicity campaign is to recall the words of Jesus, "See that you not be deceived, for many will come in My Name, saying, 'I am He,' and 'The time has come.' Do not follow them!" (Lk. 21:8). Even though Our Lord is ultimately speaking of the Antichrist, His words have already come true many times in history.

For instance, a century ago a woman named Annie Besant, who helped found the Theosophical Society (the religious movement of the New Age), "discovered" a shy young Hindu named Jiddu Krishnamurti. She believed him to be the great World Teacher, or the "Christ" of the New Age. Even though Krishnamurti thereupon embarrassed himself on a religious tour of the United States due to his lack of religious knowledge and spiritual wisdom, he eventually gained significant support, speaking before the United Nations and being endorsed by a U. S. senator and an internationally known economist.[2] (This false messiah's "work" is continued even today by the Krishnamurti Foundation of American, headquarted in Ojai, California.[3])

We would like to believe that Christians are exempt from deception by spiritual charlatans, but history provides much contrary evidence; we might think that a somewhat cynical, technological-savvy society would automatically be suspicious of someone presenting himself as a great spiritual leader, but, sadly, this is not the case. (As the great Catholic apologist G. K. Chesterton noted, when people cease believing in something, they'll believe in anything.) Just as it was with Krishnamurti, so the "Lord Maitreya," whenever he appears, will have no difficulty gaining a following, for as St. Paul warns, "the Spirit explicitly says that in the last times some will turn away from the Faith by paying attention to deceitful spirits and demonic instructions" (1 Tim. 4:1).

How is it possible that so many will be fooled, and what means will Satan, and his agent Maitreya, use to gain the world's attention? A possible answer lies in something called "Project Blue Beam," a NASA-developed holographic capability, in which space-based laser-generating satellites can project simultaneous images to the four corners of our world.

A hologram is produced by projecting nearly identical signals at a fixed point, creating a life-like image having depth perception. The particular image to be shown may be that of the Lord Maitreya—or, for a more elaborate and convincing demonstration, different images may be used at various places in the world: Mohammed, Buddha, Krishna, and even Christ, all then morphing into one—that of Maitreya himself.

At the same time, ELF (Extra Low Frequency) waves can be sent out, creating in each person a sense that he or she is hearing the voice of God.[4] These holographs and radio frequency waves might also convince people they were seeing an alien invasion,[5] and that the only hope of "repelling" the invaders was to submit to a conveniently available "savior" such as Maitreya. In this regard, we should remember that Jesus also warned, "There will be signs in the sun, the moon, and the stars" (Lk. 21:25).

All this may sound fantastic and unbelievable, and we might well wonder how rational, intelligent people would let themselves be taken in this way. However, we need to realize this sort of thing happens all the time; people can suspend their critical reasoning abilities, yoke themselves to a charismatic leader, and act in ways contrary to their own self-interest, even to the point of engaging in self-destructive behavior. The hundreds of people who followed Jim Jones to their deaths in the People's Temple cult in 1979, the group suicide of the Heaven's Gate cult members prior to the new millennium, and the mass murder/suicide of over 400 members of a religious cult in Africa in 2000, are all reminders that there are indeed spiritual wolves who disguise themselves as shepherds—and that these charismatic frauds often have little trouble attracting a following.

One author writes, "It is conservatively estimated that there are more than five thousand destructive cults or sects in this country, *with three to five million members.* At least thirty-five to fifty percent of their members are former Catholics, [only] a few of whom retain their ties to the Church."[6] Some cults, such as Scientology or Dianetics (founded by the science fiction writer L. Ron Hubbard) make no claim to be Christian,[7] but many others use Christian terminology so as to deceive potential members, while also claiming to "perfect" or complete the Bible, to escape from a corrupted Christianity, or to "fulfill" Christ's original vision for His people.

Some of the more famous religious cults include Christian Science, the Jehovah's Witnesses, Mormonism, the Worldwide Church of God, and the Rev. Sun Myung Moon's Unification Church (the "Moonies"). There are also thousands of smaller, localized cults, whose self-appointed leaders, under a veneer of Christianity, deceptively recruit members and use mind-control techniques to indoctrinate them and compel their allegiance.[8] Some of these figures are likeable and believable, while others are truly bizarre;[9] all of them are false shepherds, and thus spiritually dangerous.

Whether or not someone calling himself the Lord Maitreya appears in the near future, we must remain alert and on guard—for as Scripture warns, Satan and his servants can disguise themselves as angels of light (2 Cor. 11:14), and there will always be false teachers trying to deceive God's people (2 Pt. 2:2). The Lord offers His guidance and grace to those willing to "test the spirits" (cf. 1 Jn. 4:1), and, early in the 21st century, making this effort will perhaps become more important than ever.

NOTES

[1]Paul Proctor, "Maitreya Rising," *NewsWithViews.com*, Dec. 19, 2008.

[2]Texe Marrs, *Texe Marrs' Book of New Age Cults & Religions* (Living Truth Publishers, 1990), p. 233.

[3]*Ibid.*

[4]Jim Seabourn, "What Is the Blue Beam Project?," crtisad@inland net, Aug. 19, 1998.

[5]"Project Blue Beam—God in the Clouds," www.wfin com, June 12, 2004.

[6]Rev. Lawrence J. Gesy, *Today's Destructive Cults and Movements* (Our Sunday Visitor, 1993), pp. 14-15.

[7]Marrs, *New Age Cults & Religions*, pp. 286ff.

[8]Gesy, op.cit. p. 20.

[9]For instance, in New Guinea a violent cult leader known as "the Black Jesus" terrorized remote jungle villages—by imposing a "gospel" of rape, murder, and cannibalism—until finally apprehended by authorities. In Orlando, Florida, a charismatic leader claimed "I am upstaging Jesus Christ," after his teachings caused many people to leave their traditional churches in order to follow him. Some of his disciples—who now come from over thirty countries—even brand themselves with the number 666 (the "mark of the beast," from Rev. 13:18) as a sign of their allegiance. Cf. "Perilous Times and Prophecy in Action," by Dana Smith, www.theconservativevoice.com, May 12, 2007.

Chapter 11

Danger and Disunity
Within the Church

The *Catechism of the Catholic Church* not only condemns divination, astrology, magic or sorcery, and other such practices (par. 2116-2117) falling within the realm of the New Age Movement; it also states that the right to religious freedom is not "a moral license to adhere to error" (par. 2108)—and error is something that religious cults, by their very nature, engage in.

Many Catholics have an almost instinctive understanding of this, and would never consider leaving the Church or changing religions, let alone becoming involved in the occult. However, there are spiritual dangers which can threaten even solid Catholics. Some of these are obvious: temptations to complacency, religious laxness or laziness, tepidity, hypocrisy, smugness, a judgmental spirit, and a spirit of self-satisfaction, along with pride and the other seven deadly sins.

All these things can weaken our faith and cause us to become like salt that has lost its flavor. Jesus warns that such salt will be thrown out and trampled underfoot (Mt. 5:13), and He also admonishes us that merely going through the motions of faith will not be sufficient to merit entry into His Kingdom (Mt. 7:21-27). However, there is yet another grave spiritual danger that many Catholics fall into: that of trying to remake the Church in their own image, or insisting it change according to their beliefs and preferences—thereby giving a higher priority to their own desires than to the Church's teachings.[1] This usually takes one of two extreme forms: an ultra-traditionalist approach, which we might label "Catholic Pharisaism," and a willingness to compromise, ignore, or deny almost any Church teaching so as to fit in with the modern world, an attitude we might call "Catholicism Lite."

In regard to the first extreme, the Pharisees were, of course, a religious group within 1st century Judaism who insisted upon scrupulously perfect obedience to even the smallest part of the Law of Moses—even though many of them failed to live up to the spirit of the Law, and instead sought to use religion for their own selfish purposes. For this reason, Jesus criticized them severely for their hypocrisy (cf. Mt. 23:1-36; Mk. 7:6-13). One could say that a form of Catholic Pharisaism exists today, for there are some extreme traditionalists within the Church who not only reject the legitimacy and teachings of the Second Vatican Council, but whose opposition to the changes it brought about have—most notably in the case of the late Archbishop Marcel Lefebvre and his followers—led to outright schism.[2]

These ultra-traditionalists are not only said to be "more Catholic than the Pope," but in some cases they disdain or actually reject papal authority. Indeed, there are even some who are "sedevacantists," from the Latin expression *sede vacante*, which means "the see is vacant"—in other words, they believe the Holy See, or papal throne, is empty.[3] Such persons claim that the Popes of the last fifty years or so (e.g., ever since the death of Pius XII in 1958) have been invalidly elected, or impostors, or somehow spiritually disqualified from leading the true Church. (Persons believing this, of course, are conveniently excused from obeying any papal pronouncement contradicting their own preferences or desires.)

Needless to say, Catholic Pharisaism manifests a judgmental spirit, along with disobedience and hypocrisy; just as bad, if not worse, it also evinces a profound lack of faith—for persons adopting this perspective forget that Jesus promised His followers that the gates of hell would not prevail against the Church (Mt. 16:18), that the Holy Spirit would guide the Church to all truth (Jn. 16:13), and that He would remain with the Church always (Mt. 28:20).

(When we refer to Catholic Pharisaism, of course, we're most definitely *not* referring to traditional Catholics who happen to prefer the Latin, or Tridentine, Mass, who feel distress over much that happened after Vatican II, or who sometimes express their disappointment with the Pope or other Church leaders; rather, we're talking about religious radicals who claim such things as *only* the Latin Mass is valid, that Vatican II was an illegitimate Council not inspired or protected by the Holy Spirit, and that there hasn't been a true Pope since Pius XII. These extreme positions put their adherents outside the main stream of Catholicism—and that's a very spiritually dangerous place to be.)

The phenomenon of "Catholicism Lite" is at the opposite end of the spectrum; it's also sometimes referred to as "Cafeteria Catholicism," in which—rather than adhering to all the beliefs and teachings of the Church, people go about picking and choosing which rules and teachings they'll accept, while ignoring or rejecting those they find unpalatable and undesirable—much as a person will select certain things, but not others, at a cafeteria. Thus, religion becomes a matter of cultural identity or of personal preference, not genuine faith and a commitment to seeking the truth. Correspondingly, the concepts of obedience to legitimate authority, personal sacrifice, and spiritual and moral accountability, are downplayed or set aside entirely.

In the late 1960s and early 1970s, many revolutionary things occurred at the diocesan or parish level, all done in the so-called "spirit of Vatican II"—when in fact the Council Fathers never authorized, let alone imagined, such radical changes. Examples include the unceremonious removal of statues and other religious art work from churches, the complete abandonment of Latin as a liturgical language, the enthusiastic but poorly-done renovation of churches, excessive and illegitimate liturgical experimentation, the wholesale withdrawal by thousands of priests and nuns from their traditional ministries and spiritual duties (followed, in many cases, by the eventual relinquishing of their vocations and sometimes even their faith), the denial—or at least, the downplaying—of many traditional Catholic teachings, and the virtual elimination of all content and substance from much religious education. (This last point, probably more than any of the others, accounts for the abysmal religious illiteracy among many adult Catholics today, along with their tenuous allegiance to the Church.)

"Catholicism Lite" is a logical outgrowth of the heresy of Modernism, which denies the existence of absolute truth and the reliability of Scripture, and claims that religion must be "updated" (that is, cleansed of all its supernatural elements) in order to make it "relevant" to modern men and women.[4] The successful organization and promotion of widespread dissent to Pope Paul VI's encyclical *Humanae Vitae* in 1968 opened the floodgates, and several generations of theologians convinced themselves it was their right and even duty to doubt, question, and indeed, oppose every pronouncement of the Church's magisterium.

Some orders of religious women rebelled against the "patriarchal leadership" of the Church—to the point that many of their members crossed over to outright heresy and the practice of occult rituals and goddess worship.[5] (This, of course, gives us a deeper appreciation for the far greater number of faithful female and male religious in the Church.) Few lay Catholics have become as radical (or, we might say, theologically unhinged) as certain religious orders did, but millions have become secularized—that is, instead of being salt and light for our society, they themselves have been greatly influenced by some of the less-honorable aspects of American culture.

Some Protestant denominations in the United States have already entered into a process of inevitable and irreversible decline in membership and influence due to their abandonment of traditional Christian beliefs and morals.[6] While the Catholic Church has Christ's promise that it will overcome its enemies and share in His victory, that promise doesn't apply to those Catholics who forsake the Church, whether formally or otherwise; only those who remain united to the successor of St. Peter are assured of remaining part of the Body of Christ.

The two opposite extremes of Catholic Pharisaism and Catholicism Lite are each quite capable of leading people astray—for both are manifestations of pride, the most dangerous of all sins (and the one which was Lucifer's undoing). One attitude says, "I refuse to accept any changes made after the papacy of Pius XII; everything in the Church I don't approve of is obviously invalid." The other attitude says, "No one is going to tell me what I must believe and how I must behave—especially when it comes to my money, my sex life, and my politics."

Jesus, however, says, "Come to Me . . . and *learn* from Me for I am meek and humble of heart" (Mt. 11:28-29). The only possible safeguard against the deadly sin of pride is a spirit of humility, and a sense of meekness and docility, which is the ability to admit that one doesn't know everything. True humility and meekness are demonstrated by a willingness to continue learning from the Church on moral and religious matters, and an openness to changing one's thinking when appropriate.

Within Catholicism, the mainstream is very broad and accommodating: there is room for those who prefer the traditional Latin Mass, and those more comfortable with the contemporary (or *Novus Ordo*) Mass; those who prefer the Rosary and other traditional devotions, and those who don't find them all that spiritually helpful; those who prefer traditional or gothic-style church buildings, and those who feel more at ease with modern architecture; those who prefer Gregorian chant, and those who like the St. Louis Jesuits; those who will only receive Holy Communion on the tongue, and those who prefer to receive the Host in their hands; those who kneel behind the screen to confess their sins, and those who sit and talk to the priest face to face; those who like Forty Hours and Perpetual Help devotions, and those who'd get more out of a charismatic prayer group meeting; those who place a lot of value on alleged private revelations, and those who pay no attention to them; those who would prefer taking part in a Corpus Christi procession, and those who'd rather participate in a protest march or a peace and justice rally; and those who read *The Wanderer*, along with those who subscribe to *The National Catholic Reporter*. All of these are legitimate options; what *isn't* legitimate is for any of us to insist that ours is the only correct way of being Catholic, and that those who disagree with us are obviously unfaithful Catholics or second-class members of the Church.

There are times when Church authorities have to exercise discipline, dissolve certain groups or associations, or declare various ideas and practices illegitimate or even heretical. However, Our Lord's parable of the Pharisee and the publican (Lk. 18:9-14), and the story of the woman caught in adultery (Jn. 8:1-11), warn us not to give into the temptation of judging others or considering ourselves superior to them; as Jesus says, only those who humble themselves can expect to be exalted in His Kingdom (Lk.14:7-14).

The spiritually dangerous attitudes and beliefs we've been

examining in these last few chapters—a growing unwillingness to make a commitment to a particular Christian religion on the part of many Americans, the claims of the New Age Movement to unlock the godlike potential in each one of us, and the positions of Catholic Pharisaism and Catholicism Lite—all manifest a spirit of pride and even of outright rebellion against God's laws and the teachings of His Son's Church.

Lucifer was the greatest of the angels, but his pride was his undoing (cf. Is. 14:12-15), and ever since he was cast out of Heaven, Lucifer—now known as Satan—has warred against humanity (Rev. 12:7-9; 17). Nothing pleases him more than to trip us up by various temptations—especially that of pride. That's why St. Peter urges, "All of you, clothe yourselves with humility in your dealings with one another, for 'God opposes the proud but bestows favor on the humble.' So humble yourselves under the mighty hand of God, that He may exalt you in due time" (1 Pt. 5:5-6). If we do our best to live this way, we will not be deceived or led astray, and our faith will be strengthened and rewarded.

NOTES

[1]Gallup's 2006 – 2008 Values and Beliefs surveys indicate that "even among committed Catholics, a slim majority seem to be at odds with the Church's positions on premarital sex, embryonic stem-cell research, divorce, and the death penalty." The number of *church-going* Catholics (those who attend Mass weekly or almost every week) who regard abortion as morally acceptable is 24%. For the issue of sex between an unmarried man and woman, 53% regard it as morally acceptable; for having a baby outside marriage, the figure is 48%; for homosexual relations, the figure is 44%; for divorce, the figure is 63%; and for medical research using stem cells from human embryos, the figure is 53%. From "Catholics Similar to Mainstream on Abortion, Stem Cells," quoted in *Christifidelis*, May 1, 2009.

[2]Patrick Madrid and Pete Vere, *More Catholic than the Pope* (Our Sunday Visitor, 2004), p. 9.

[3]Rev. Richard John Neuhaus, *Catholic Matters: Confusion, Controversy, and the Splendor of the Truth* (Basic Books, 2006), p. 178.

[4]For a discussion of Modernism and its pernicious effects on the Church,

see *The Signs of the Times*, by Fr. Richard W. Gilsdorf (Star of the Bay Press, 2008); *What Went Wrong With Vatican II*, by Ralph McInerny (Sophia Institute Press, 1998); *Christ Denied — Origins of the Present-Day Problems in the Church*, by Rev. Paul Wickens (TAN Books & Publishers, 1982); *Catholicism Overturned*, by Fr. Malachi Martin (Triumph Communications, 2001); *The Desolate City*, by Anne Roche Muggeridge (Harper & Row, 1986); *A Crisis of Truth*, by Ralph Martin (Servant Books, 1982); and my own *Catholicism in Crisis* (Queenship Publishing, 2008).

[5]Donna Steichen, *Ungodly Rage: The Hidden Face of Catholic Feminism* (Ignatius Press, 1991), pp. 29ff.

[6]David Carlin, *The Decline & Fall of the Catholic Church in America* (Sophia Institute Press, 2003), pp. 187ff.

Section D

Is A Religious Persecution Coming?

Chapter 12

Signs of a Coming Persecution

If it's true the blood of martyrs is the seed of future Christians—as the 3rd century Christian leader Tertullian asserted—then many seeds are being planted in today's world. According to one estimate, hundreds of Christians are dying for their faith each day, while several hundred million others face severe restrictions on practicing their faith;[1] another estimate suggests that a thousand Christians a day give their lives for Christ.[2]

Persecution is frequently involved in living the Gospel; there are many Scriptural references to religious persecution,[3] including the warning in 2 Tim. 3:12 that "all who want to live religiously in Christ Jesus will be persecuted." Sometimes this assault on believers is quite severe, as is currently the case in Communist China and North Korea, or even genocidal, as in the efforts of the Sudanese government to wipe out the Christian inhabitants of southern Sudan. Quite often, however, followers of Christ are harassed in a less-threatening, but still significant, way. The hostility of the world should be no surprise to us, for as one evangelical author noted, we are now living in the "post-Christian era" (especially in Western Europe and the United States).[4]

In 1980, Pope John Paul II, in an informal statement to a group of Catholics, said:

We must be prepared to undergo great trials in the not-too-

distant future; trials that will require us to give up even our lives, and a total gift of self to Christ and for Christ.
Through your prayers and mine, it is possible to alleviate this tribulation, but it is no longer possible to avert it, because it is only in this way that the Church can be effectively renewed. How many times, indeed, has the renewal of the Church been effected in blood?
This time, again, it will not be otherwise.[5]

If, to think the previously unthinkable, a religious persecution may actually be coming to the United States, we have to ask ourselves: Why might such a persecution occur? What reasons would God have for allowing His Church to be assaulted by its enemies in an open and direct manner?

History can be instructive here. There were limited persecutions of Christianity by the Roman Empire during the Church's first two centuries of existence (such as Nero's attack on the Christians of Rome in the mid-60s, during which St. Peter and St. Paul both were martyred), but the first major, Empire-wide assault on the Church didn't occur until 250, during the reign of the Emperor Decius. St. Cyprian, Bishop of Carthage, survived this persecution by going into hiding (though he later died as a martyr in 258 during Emperor Valerian's attack on the Church). After the persecution ended, the saint reflected on why the Lord allowed it to occur.

According to St. Cyprian, there were three reasons for the persecution: (1) Christians could not spiritually withstand an extended period of peace and prosperity; (2) in every level of the Church, believers had fallen into materialism and worldly concerns; and (3) because they were infected with materialism, they lost their zeal for the Faith.[6]

Can anyone seriously claim this same situation doesn't exist among Catholics and other Christians in present-day America?

Another ominous lesson from history involves a comparison of Germany in the 1930s and the United States in the early 21st century. In his book *Storm Warning: The Coming Persecution of Christians and Traditionalists in America*, Christian author Don McAlvany lists these parallels: (1) a preoccupation with death (including euthanasia in Germany, and abortion and now also euthanasia in the U. S.); (2) the promulgation of thousands of laws, rules,

_____ .egulations (making it theoretically possible to find almost anyone guilty of some crime); (3) a preoccupation with environmentalism and animal rights (in which nature is given a higher value than the needs of human beings); (4) an unhealthy interest in the supernatural (manifested by an occultic dimension in the Third Reich, and by the influence of the New Age Movement on American society); (5) a deliberate decision to ignore the Constitution (which Hitler did repeatedly, and which the U. S. government—especially the judiciary—is doing today); (6) the rejection of one's national heritage (in which earlier heroes and ideals are downgraded or even discredited); and (7) the imposition of strict gun control laws (making it difficult or impossible for citizens to resist government tyranny).[7]

Certainly America, for all her sins, is in no way comparable to Nazi Germany; nevertheless, history proves that a highly civilized society can be horribly transformed in a sudden and dramatic manner under the right conditions—and it's foolish to assume the United States is somehow exempt from this truth.

According to Mr. McAlvany, evangelical Christians, faithful Catholics, and persons upholding traditional values are very unpopular with, or even hated by, such influential groups as political liberals, secular humanists, some (not all) atheists, the gay lobby, the abortion industry and its supporters, radical environmentalists, Communists, New World Order supporters, Satanists and some other practitioners of the occult, and many New Agers.[8] Furthermore, some commentators have noted a desire on the part of global socialists to gain control over the world's population, wealth, and resources; this is a key (though often hidden) element in the agenda of the movement toward the so-called New World Order.[9] History shows that when individuals or groups with a radical cultural and social agenda gain political power, they naturally use that power to implement their desired changes, while taking steps to prevent effective resistance by their opponents—either by restricting their rights, or by persecuting them directly or indirectly.

Experts generally agree that a persecution unfolds in five stages. First of all, the targeted group is *stereotyped or stigmatized*, making it an easier target of bigotry, slander, and abuse. Then the group is *marginalized*, or pushed out of the mainstream of society,

by efforts to reduce its moral authority and influence. T
group is *vilified*—that is, viciously attacked and blamed for society ᵕ
problems. In the fourth stage, the group is *criminalized* through
the use of increasing legal restrictions upon its membership and
activities. The final stage is marked by outright *persecution*. Some
commentators claim that America is currently in stage three of
this process, and moving into stage four[10]—and there is abundant
evidence to support this view.

In the past, there have been numerous cases of discrimination
or even police brutality against peaceful pro-life demonstrators
here in the United States. For instance, in Atlanta a minister's
jaw was dislocated during his arrest, and he suffered a concus-
sion when thrown into a police van, but he was denied medical
treatment for several hours. A Mass being said for imprisoned
pro-life demonstrators was interrupted by the authorities, and the
detained priest was put into solitary confinement. In Pittsburgh,
arrested pro-lifers were denied contact with their attorneys and
refused food and water; three of them later had to be hospitalized
for dehydration.

In Los Angeles, kneeling non-violent demonstrators were lifted
up by their nostrils; others were assaulted with nunchucks (which
are actually illegal in California). In West Hartford, Connecticut,
a priest in a holding cell was no longer recognizable after being
beaten by police; on the same day, thirty-one other arrested demonstrators suffered serious injury inflicted by police officers. (*The
Hartford Courant*, the local newspaper, responded to this outrage
with an editorial praising the police for *showing restraint* in handling
the demonstrators.[11])

The suffering of pro-life activists is largely ignored in the media,
and their legal rights often go unprotected. In 1994, for instance,
the Supreme Court ruled that the federal racketeering statutes
(RICO) could be used against pro-life demonstrators praying in
front of abortion clinics. These statutes—originally intended for
use against organized crime—allow the imposition of treble dam-
ages against anyone engaged in a "criminal conspiracy."[12]

However, it's not only the right-to-life movement that's under assault; freedom of speech for religious believers is no longer
universally respected. One homosexual activist stated, "Opinions

85

are protected under the First Amendment, but when negative opinions come out of a person's fist, mouth, or pen to intentionally hurt others, *that's when their opinions should no longer be protected"* (emphasis added).[13] There's a growing movement to redefine religious opposition to homosexual behavior as a "hate crime," which would lead to a situation similar to that already existing in Canada: religious broadcasters who refer to Romans 1 (which contains a condemnation of homosexual activity) can be legally charged with engaging in unethical practices.[14]

In his book *Speechless: Silencing the Christians*, Rev. Donald E. Wildmon (a Methodist minister who founded the American Family Association) writes:

> For decades, a growing number of the American elite—the people who manage the media and mold the culture, run our great colleges and corporations, and train our lawyers and judges—has been gripped by a growing anger, now becoming a raging fury, against any person, group, church, or institution committed to Christian moral teachings. Like the [ancient] Romans, these people hear Christ's truth as an accusation. They even see Christ's love on the cross as their condemnation. And strangely enough, they see Christian families not as witnesses for Christ but as witnesses against them. . . . The coalition of liberal secularists and homosexual activists—let's call them "homosecularists" for short—have some very real goals that they know they can achieve only by driving Christians out of public life.[15]

As part of this process, the constitutionally-guaranteed religious rights of Christians are no longer automatically recognized in court, as numerous instances demonstrate. Some judges have prohibited the possession or distribution of Bibles or religious literature, and any form of witnessing or praying, in public buildings, parks, and street corners; huge fines, and even imprisonment, have been imposed on violators. One Christian was sentenced to thirty days in jail for praying in a New York City courtroom, and a judge threatened to imprison for thirty days anyone praying in or near his courtroom during a trial of pro-life demonstrators in Buffalo.[16]

In 2006, a private group in Washington D. C. placed a large

granite monument of the Ten Commandments on its own prop-erty—which happened to be located directly across the street from the U. S. Supreme Court. Local officials immediately ordered the monument removed on "zoning" grounds, threatening to seize the property unless their diktat was obeyed. That same year, in a rul-ing on a lawsuit filed by the "Americans United for Separation of Church and State," a federal judge ordered the Newton Correction Facility in Iowa to remove a Bible-based prison program (and even ordered the Bible group to re-pay the state of Iowa over $1.5 million for its "crime" of inflicting Christianity upon the prisoners). Also in 2006, at "Ground Zero" in Manhattan, officials decided to remove a steel cross (made by two intersecting beams from the rubble of the World Trade Center) for fear someone might be offended by this religious symbol; as they explained, "it's a delicate issue."

Judicial officials have shown an increasing willingness to ignore the rights and freedoms of religious believers. The New York Court of Appeals ordered, in 2006, all Catholic institutions in the state to provide contraceptive coverage for their female employees—even though this act would violate Catholic teaching. During that same year, the 6th Court of Appeals in Cincinnati overrode the religious objections of a Baptist prison chaplain and ruled that he must per-mit a practicing homosexual to direct his prison choir.[17]

The Archdiocese of Boston was forced to close its adoption pro-gram because the state of Massachusetts required Catholic Chari-ties, like every other adoption agency, to allow same-sex couples to adopt. The Archdiocese was willing to provide referrals for such couples to other agencies, but that wasn't enough for the state.[18] In California, fertility doctors were sued because their religious objections caused them to refuse in-vitro fertilization to a lesbian couple;[19] also, a Methodist organization in New Jersey lost part of its tax-exempt status because it wouldn't allow lesbian couples to be joined in a civil union ceremony on its property.[20] In a similar case, a lesbian couple filed a complaint with New Mexico's Human Rights Commission against a wedding photographer because she declined to take photos of their civil union ceremony.[21]

Other branches of government are also increasingly disinclined to respect the rights and beliefs of Christians. The San Francisco Board of Supervisors passed a non-binding resolution denouncing the Catholic Church for its opposition to homosexual adoption, calling the Catholic teaching on homosexuality "hateful," "discriminatory," "insulting," and "ignorant."[22] A double standard has been manifested by lawmakers in New York State and California in regard to the sexual molestation of minors: they've attempted to remove the statute of limitations for allegations against Catholic Church personnel, while keeping it in effect for employees of the government school system (even though a leading authority on the subject estimated that "the physical abuse of students in [public or government] schools is likely more than 100 times the abuse of priests").[23] Early in 2009, a bill was proposed in the Connecticut legislature that would have removed financial control of Catholic parishes from their priests and the diocesan bishop; fortunately, this measure died because of widespread negative publicity and opposition.[24]

All too often, though, Catholics and other Christians are unable to protect themselves against discrimination. A man in Virginia was fired from his job at a food-processing plant—simply because his pickup truck carried a bumper sticker supporting a proposed amendment to the state constitution defining marriage as a union between one man and one woman. In Maryland, an employee of the state's transit authority board was asked about his views on homosexuality on a cable television talk show. Speaking as a private citizen—not as a transit employee—he said, "I'm a Roman Catholic. Homosexual behavior is, in my view, deviant." That was enough to get him fired by the governor of Maryland.[25]

Another trap for unwary Christians is that of "political correctness." This modern fad, which is in conflict with Scripture and Church teaching in several important areas (particularly the biblical teachings on sin, personal accountability, and sexual morality), has made many college and high school, and even elementary school, campuses hostile to Christianity. Quite a few government schools forbid the use of the terms "Christmas" and "Easter," and students—and even some teachers—have been disciplined for daring to read a personal copy of the Bible during silent reading times.

At many universities, Christian students have their faith mocked by professors and fellow students; since 2000, at least fifty universities have expelled, or attempted to expel, Christian student groups from campus.[26] One student who declined to sign a professor's petition expressing support for adoption by same-sex couples was investigated by the university's social work department and changed with ethics violations; another who stated her agreement with the Christian view of sexuality and marriage was reprimanded by the university for contradicting its solidarity with the "GLBT community." A male student who spoke in favor of a book that referred to homosexual behavior as sinful was accused of sexual harassment, and several professors filed formal charges against him.[27]

Negative stereotyping of Catholics, Christians, and other adherents of traditional values, is routinely practiced in much of the entertainment and communications industry; one news show host[28] said, on national television, that anyone opposing the Freedom of Choice Act (FOCA), which would eliminate every restriction on abortion, is "a terrorist." The news media—both in the United States and in Europe—is increasingly disinclined to respect the leadership and moral teachings of the Catholic Church. According to the Italian Jesuit magazine *La Civilta Cattolica*, "Catholics in Italy and Europe know very well that a preconceived hostility exists against Church doctrine, especially in the field of ethics. . . [the mass media] which is the voice of powerful forces and interests, is an excellent propagator of this hostility."[29]

In regard to popular culture, noted film critic Michael Medved has observed, "In the ongoing war on traditional values, the assault on organized faith represents the front to which the entertainment industry has most clearly committed itself."[30] Medved (in his book *Hollywood vs. America*) is only one of several commentators who've chronicled the denigration of Christians, and Christian values, in movies and television; Catholics and other religious believers are frequently portrayed as narrow-minded, hypocritical religious zealots, unwilling or incapable of contributing anything worthwhile to modern society.[31]

American culture was once permeated with Christianity, but signs of a growing hostility to religious values are becoming more difficult to ignore. Sacrilegious attacks on religion are becoming commonplace; a professor in Minnesota announced he was desecrating stolen Eucharistic Hosts, and a young man appeared on YouTube destroying Hosts by frying, boiling, or flushing them.[32] Also, Christians have been intimidated after voting in favor of state initiatives defending traditional marriage, requiring parental notification before a minor's abortion, or opposing physician-assisted suicide;[33] gay activists have even used Google Maps to discover the home addresses of donors to traditional causes.[34]

Catholics had to struggle for much of our nation's history to be accepted as equal and trustworthy participants in the American democratic experiment; having come out of their "ghetto" only a few decades ago, it's not surprising many of them (especially bishops and priests) don't want to rock the boat by sticking up for their rights or being involved in any type of controversy. At the same time, Protestants have always been part of the dominant majority in U. S. society, and that experience and mentality can make it very difficult for them to adjust to changing realities. Nevertheless, major changes are under way, and it's foolish for religious believers to deny or ignore this growing problem of hostility to our country's Judeo-Christian heritage and founding ideals. America, which was once "one nation under God," is increasingly becoming "one nation *rebelling against* God"—and outright religious persecution may well become part of this spiritually and socially self-destructive trend.

NOTES

[1]Paul Marshall, *Their Blood Cries Out* (Word Publishing, 1997), p. 254. According to Marshall, commentator David B. Barrett defines a martyr as "a believer in Christ who loses his or her life prematurely in a situation of witness as a result of human hostility" (pp. 254-255). Marshall states, "In general we can say that currently, two hundred fifty million Christians are persecuted for their faith, and a further four hundred million live under non-trivial restrictions on their religious liberty" (p. 255).

[2]Don McAlvany, *Storm Warning: The Coming Persecution of Christians and Traditionalists in America* (Hearthstone Publishing, 1999), p. 10.

[3]See, for instance, Mt. 5:11; Mt. 5:44-45; Mt. 10:16; Mt. 13:20-21; Mk. 10:29-

30; Mk. 13:9-13; Jn. 15:18-21; Jn. 16:1-2; Acts 5:41; Rm. 8:35; Rm. 12:14; 2 Cor. 4:8-10; 2 Cor. 12:10; 1 Th. 1:6-7; Heb. 10:32-39; 1 Pt. 4:12-19; and Rev. 6:9-11.

[4]McAlvany, op.cit. p. 11. This trend is especially pronounced in Europe. An article called "EU Parliament Removes Religious Exemption: Churches Could be Forced to Perform Same-Sex 'Marriage,'" Hilary White on *LifeSiteNews.com* (quoted in *Catholic Family News*, May 2009), states, "Changes made in April in the EU Anti-Discrimination Directive could force Christian and other religious groups to perform homosexual 'marriages' and allow non-believers to receive Communion and other sacraments in their churches. The directive was adopted by the EU Parliament on April 2, by 360 votes in favor and 227 votes against and will apply to all organizations offering a service to the public, including hospitals, charities, businesses, prisons, and churches. . . . Similar legislation passed in Britain under the Tony Blair government resulted in the closure of several Catholic adoption agencies after the government refused to allow a religious exemption."

[5]Regis Scanlon, "Flood and Fire," *Homiletic & Pastoral Review,* April 1994.

[6]Desmond A. Birch, *Trial, Tribulation & Triumph* (Queenship Publishing, 1996), pp. 299-300.

[7]McAlvany, op.cit. pp. 184ff.

[8]*Ibid.,* p. 12.

[9]Gurudas, *Treason: The New World Order* (Cassandra Press, 1996), p. 27. Gurudas (a pseudonym) writes: "There is an intimate relationship between socialism and those promoting a new world order with a one world government. . . . Ultimately socialism is a greater threat than is communism, because socialism uses a gradual and insidious approach to achieve total control over the people, while the objectives of communism are more obvious. . . . A constant strategy is to claim that governments must work together to solve the major problems of the day. Supposedly, it is beyond the ability of individual nations to solve today's problems, so there must be a coordinated world strategy. . . . The plan is to create a world army, world court, world currency, world bank, and world tax. Each state will have only a lightly armed police force, while private gun ownership will end" (p. 27).

[10]McAlvany, op.cit. p. 285.

[11]Gailfred Boller Sweetland, "Police Brutality: No Press Coverage," supplement to the *Catholic League Newsletter*, Vol. 16, no. 9 (Fall 1989).

[12]McAlvany, op.cit. p. 251.

[13]Ed Vitagliano, "Homosexual Activists 'Getting Tough' With Their Opponents," *American Family Association Journal*, Nov./Dec. 1999, p. 4.

[14]Frank York, "Is Christianity a 'Hate Crime'?," *WorldNetDaily.com*, Dec. 3, 1999.

[15]Rev. Donald E. Wildmon, *Speechless: Silencing the Christians* (Richard

Vigilante Books, 2009), p. 13.

[16]McAlvany, pp. 244-245.

[17]John-Henry Western, "2006 Losses of Religious Freedom Should Make American Christians Wake Up," *LifeSiteNews.com*, Jan. 17, 2007.

[18]Mark Hemingway, "Gay Abandon," *National Review*, July 14, 2008.

[19]*Ibid.* This procedure, of course, is not morally acceptable to the Church, but the situation itself serves as another illustration of Christians finding themselves in court due to their religious and moral beliefs.

[20]Jennifer Roback Morse, "Same-Sex 'Marriage' and the Persecution of Civil Society," *NCRegister.com*, June 8 – 14, 2008.

[21]*Ibid.*

[22]Western, op. cit.

[23]"Politics of Sex Abuse in New York," *Catalyst*, May 2009.

[24]Ken Dixon, "How Catholics, Bishops Killed Senate Bill," *ConnPost.com*, March 15, 2009. It should be noted, however, that after the bill died, Bishop William Lori of Bridgeport was informed by an examiner at the Connecticut Office of State Ethics that the Diocese's organized opposition constituted a case of illegal lobbying—making the Church subject to potential civil penalties—for the Diocese had not registered as a lobbyist (an act which would have brought "intrusive oversight and regulation by the state," in the Bishop's words). Fortunately, this bureaucratic power grab also came to naught. See Bishop Lori's letter in *The Catholic Family News*, "Letters to the Editor," July 2009, p. 27.

[25]Ed Vitagliano, "Silence!," *American Family Association Journal*, May 2007, p. 15.

[26]David French, "Expelling God from the University," *Catalyst*, May 2006.

[27]*Ibid.*

[28]MSNBC's Chris Matthews.

[29]*La Civlta Cattolica*, May 2, 2009, as quoted in *The Michigan Catholic*, May 8, 2009.

[30]McAlvany, op.cit. p. 278.

[31]Limbaugh, op.cit. pp. 265ff.

[32]Michael H. Brown, "Beyond Sacrilege, Attacks on Church Now Aimed at Its Most Profound Level," *Spirit.Daily.com*.

[33]"Hot Election Issues Ignite; Bigotry Flares," *Catalyst*, Dec. 2008.

[34]Chuck Colson, "Mapping Political Persecution," *Crosswalk.com*, Feb. 24, 2009.

Chapter 13

Government Plans
and Preparations

The year 2010 will be a milestone in human history: by that point in time, there will be *one billion* transistors per *every person* on earth, each costing only one ten-millionth of a cent.[1] The unimaginably massive use of RFID chips, most of them networked together (in automobiles, roadways, appliances, cell phones, drivers' licenses, credit cards, SMART cards, pipelines, doorways of public buildings and private homes, items of clothing, pharmaceuticals, livestock and pets, and—sooner or later—human beings) will allow an unprecedented degree of ongoing and virtually inescapable surveillance. In addition, high-speed cameras are now used at red lights, railroad crossings, pedestrian crosswalks, shopping malls and convenience stores, and in too many other locations to mention, with many of them available for the use of facial recognition technology.[2]

It's becoming extremely difficult for people to hide themselves or keep a low profile. Today the average American is listed in at least a dozen different government databases, which contain his or her tax, financial, medical, police, educational, and military records; these can easily be used to assemble accurate profiles, including—by means of banking and personal checking records—that person's religious and political preferences.[3] The FBI is creating a national database of the DNA samples of millions of U. S. citizens,[4] and—combined with the above-mentioned technological surveillance grid—the last remaining shreds of privacy will disappear for much of the world's population.

This pervasive violation of human freedom and dignity will undoubtedly be justified in the name of national security, using the need to fight terrorism and crime as an excuse. However, as Benjamin Franklin wisely noted over two centuries ago, those who sacrifice liberty for the sake of security deserve to be neither free nor secure. Civil liberty is at risk when the same persons or branches of government charged with fighting crime also have the power to define criminal activity—and America is rapidly heading toward this frightening state of affairs.

Many U. S. citizens are now "criminals" without knowing or intending it, for Congress passes almost 2500 new laws per year (most containing both civil and criminal penalties). The government holds that we have no excuse for unknowingly violating the law, for we've been "legally advised" via *The Federal Register* (consisting of 85,000 pages of new laws each year). This impossible standard theoretically gives officials a reason to prosecute (or persecute?) almost anyone.[5] Religious believers could easily become victims of hostile government attention. Prior to the year 2000, for instance, the FBI's "Project Megiddo" report listed religious organizations and cults supposedly linked to terrorist groups—though it admitted it had uncovered very little evidence of specific threats to domestic security.[6]

Early in 2009, the Department of Homeland Security issued a report warning of potential civil unrest caused by "right wing extremists"; included in this category were "groups and individuals that are dedicated to a single issue, such as abortion . . . ," i.e., anyone involved in the Right to Life Movement. (A further DHS report, issued just a few weeks later, also included anyone using alternative forms of media, such as talk radio and internet news websites.)[7]

Elaborating on this theme, the DHS has helpfully provided law enforcement agencies with warning signs of potential "terrorists." Along with opposition to abortion and same-sex marriage, there are numerous other mainstream political positions that, in a surveillance society, now raise red flags.[8] For example, Missouri law enforcement officers were warned to beware of libertarians, people who display bumper stickers, and those who fly U. S. flags; these acts may be an indication of domestic terrorism. In Virginia, a training manual for state employees included these items as "terrorist tools": binoculars, video cameras, and paper pads and notebooks. Even more absurdly, in Texas, a pamphlet by the Dept. of Public Safety lists these possible danger signs of terrorist activity: buying baby formula or beer, wearing Levi jeans, carrying identifying documents like a driver's license, and traveling with women or children.[9] Such heightened alarm on the part of national officials is not just theoretical, as the following examples prove. In May 2008, a student at a Bible college in east Texas was confronted by federal agents and accused of an "act of terror and espionage." His crime? Giving a talk to some Boy Scouts, in which he advocated educating themselves about the U. S. Constitution. In July 2007, a sheriff's deputy in North Carolina broke into the home of a married couple, assaulted them, and then arrested them for the offense of flying a U. S. flag upside down (an act which, according to the U. S. Flag Code, is *not* disrespectful, and may even be patriotic). In August 2008, a Las Vegas couple was stopped by police, detained, and searched; when the couple demanded to know why, one of the police officers pointed to the political bumper stickers on their car.[10] A resident of Washington D.C., after protesting a ruling by a district court judge, was visited at home by two U. S. Marshals and warned to watch his behavior.[11]

Also, a young man employed by a libertarian political group was detained and harassed by TSA (Transportation and Safety Administration) agents in the St. Louis airport simply for carrying $4700 in cash—proceeds from the sale of books at a conference. Though they had no legal authority to hold him without evidence of a crime, they did so for several hours (and then threatened to turn him over to the DEA, or Drug Enforcement Agency, for questioning) until an FBI agent intervened and had him released.[12]

As if all that weren't bad enough, a FEMA symposium given to firefighters and other emergency personnel in Kansas City admitted that in times of national emergency, Christians and home schoolers should be considered terrorists and treated with the "utmost suspicion and brutality."[13] (Not all forms of organized religion are unpopular with the authorities, however; in 2006 it became known that, in a nationwide FEMA program, "Clergy Response Teams" were being trained to use their influence to help "quell dissent" by urging citizens to obey the government should martial law ever be declared.[14])

In spite of the constitutional protections enumerated in the Bill of Rights, our civil liberties may very well be hanging by a thread. For instance, the Military Commissions Act of 2006 grants the president the power to identify U. S. citizens as "unlawful enemy combatants" and detain them indefinitely without charge—a convenient way for the government to round up anyone resisting illegal decrees.[15] Other proposed legislation is equally frightening, including measures to crack down on political activism,[16] compel community service by young people in government programs,[17] effectively overturn the Second Amendment,[18] give the White House power to restrict the use of the Internet by its political opponents,[18] and even prohibit Americans from growing food for themselves and their animals without government permission.[19]

Proposed legislation, of course, may never be enacted (or may later be overturned by the courts as unconstitutional), but there is no such protection from Executive Orders, which allow the president—by a stroke of a pen—to confiscate virtually all private property and suspend all civil liberties.[20] Other potential government abuses of power might involve the Drug Currency Forfeitures Act, which would likely increase the number of Americans (currently 250,000 each year) whose assets are seized by law enforcement officials,[21] and even the imposition of martial law, which could be declared in a state of emergency (real or otherwise).[22]

Some U. S. military and National Guard units have received training in crowd control, house-to-house searches, and domestic counter-terrorism measures, and the criminal enforcement agencies (the DEA, FBI, CIA, BATF, EPA, FDA, and IRS) could provide an additional 300,000 personnel for use in implementing government decrees.[23] Also, according to one journalist, "For the first time ever, the U. S. military is deploying an active duty regular Army combat unit for full-time use inside the United States to deal with emergencies, including potential civil unrest,"[24] and training exercises—using live ammunition—have been conducted by the U. S. military in dozens of American cities.[25]

Furthermore, there have been numerous confirmed reports of foreign troops—particularly from Germany and Russia—training on U. S. soil,[26] conceivably providing additional manpower for our government to use in a state of emergency (as foreign troc have fewer qualms about using force against U. S. civilians than American troops would). Indeed, there is even speculation that the recording of the GPS coordinates of every private residence in America[27]—which the government claims is merely a preparation for the 2010 census—is actually intended to make it easier for foreign troops to locate the residents of particular homes, should a government-imposed "round-up" of civilians ever be deemed necessary.

If such a large-scale round-up were to occur—whether as the result of martial law, or an actual religious persecution—where would these persons be taken? According to one report, "There [are] over 800 prison camps in the United States, all fully operational and ready to receive prisoners. They are all staffed and even surrounded by full-time guards, *but they are empty.* These camps are to be operated by FEMA (Federal Emergency Management Agency) should Martial Law need to be implemented. . . ."[28] This statement echoes other reports of a similar nature.[29]

All this evidence suggests that, should the government ever decide upon a religious persecution, most of the necessary elements are already in place. Therefore, our own preparations should also be well underway—and some important suggestions are offered in the following chapter.

NOTES

[1]"Smart Grid: Government Spying on Rural America," *RFD America,* March 8, 2009.

[2]Kurt Nimmo, "Government Prepares the Public for Cradle to Grave Surveillance," *Infowars.com,* Feb. 28, 2009. This article also notes, "implementing this intrusive technology—facial recognition cameras, RFID chips, and GPS track and tax—is part of the world government agenda, beginning with the merger of Canada, Mexico, and the Untied States, otherwise known as the North American Union. . . . The global elite will track our every move. Imposing burdensome taxes on us is only part of the agenda. The other and equally important part is the 'electronic identification for every adult in the U. S.' (and eventually the entire world), especially those who may attend anti-government rallies."

[3]*McAlvany Intelligence Advisor*, Jan. 1999, p. 5.

[4]"DNA Database Raises Fears of Big Brother," *The Orange County Register*, Oct. 12, 1998.

[5]McAlvany, *Storm Warning: The Coming Persecution of Christians and Traditionalists in America* (Hearthstone Publishing, 1999),p. 54. Also, according to Gurudas, "Another strategy is to introduce an especially egregious law or program in a less-populated state where there is less media coverage. If the law passes, it is introduced in other states. If there is great resistance, the government backs down, always watching how the people react, perhaps presenting the law in another state with certain changes" (p. 53).

[6]Kelly Patricia O'Meara, "FBI Targets 'Right Wing,'" *Insight*, Dec. 27, 1996. This article quotes Jan LaRue, the senior advisor to the Family Research Council, as saying that by this action, "The FBI is treading dangerously close to trampling on the constitutional rights of some Americans. The problem is that they are looking into peoples' beliefs with no account of actual criminal action. Putting law-abiding people of faith under suspicion without criminal conduct is wrong."

[7]Tom DeWeese, "The Department of Homeland Security is a 'Man-Caused Disaster,'" *The DeWeese Report* (June 2009), p. 1.

[8]According to the DHS, any of these positions—if leading to any level of civil disobedience—would constitute a terrorist act: concern over the economic policies of the Obama Administration; criticism of NAFTA (North American Free Trade Agreement) and SPP (Security and Prosperity Partnership); belief in the "end times"; stockpiling food, weapons, and ammunition; opposition to illegal immigration; opposition to the New World Order, the United Nations, and global governance; opposition to a loss of U. S. prestige; fear of Communism; and the use of the internet or any type of alternative media to express any of these ideas. At the same time, actual acts of terrorism by Muslim extremists will, in the interests of political correctness, instead be referred to as "man-caused disasters." *Ibid.*, p. 2.

It's interesting to note that, while serving as Attorney General in the Clinton Administration, Janet Reno gave this definition of religious cultists on the TV news show *Sixty Minutes*:

A cultist is one who has a strong belief in the Bible and the Second Coming of Christ; who frequently attends Bible studies; who has a high level of financial giving to a Christian cause; who home schools for their children; who has accumulated survival foods and has a strong belief in the 2nd Amendment; and who distrusts big government. Any of these may qualify [a person as a cultist] but certainly more than one would cause us to look at this person as a threat, and his family as being in a risk situation that qualified for government interference (*Sixty Minutes*, June 26, 1994).

One cannot help but recall the words of Jesus: "If you belonged to the world, the world would love its own; but because you do not belong to the world, and I have chosen you out of the world, the world hates you" (Jn. 15:19).

⁹Paul Joseph Watson, Kurt Nimmo & Alex Jones, "Police Trained Nationwide that Informed Americans Are Domestic Terrorists," *PrisonPlanet.com*, March 13, 2009, p. 1.

¹⁰*Ibid.*, p. 3. U. S. citizens who may find themselves in a similar situation can find advice on how to defend their constitutional rights at www.flexyourrights.com.

¹¹*The American Sentinel*, May 2009.

¹²www.brasschecktv.com.page.589.html. Unknown to the TSA agents, the young man was recording their interrogation on his cell phone. He was calm and respectful, and several times asked, "Am I required by law to answer that question?," followed by "If I am required by law, I will be happy to answer that question." The agents were unable to answer him affirmatively, but continued their harassment, until—while preparing to take him to the local police station—the FBI agent quietly spoke to them, and then told the young man he was free to go.

¹³Watson, Nimmo, & Jones, op.cit. pp. 2-3.

¹⁴*Ibid.*, pp. 3-4. According to the article, "It was related to the Pastors that quarantines, martial law and forced relocation were a problem for state authorities when enforcing federal mandates due to the 'cowboy mentality' of citizens standing up for their property and second amendment rights as well as farmers defending their crops and livestock from seizure. It was stressed that the Pastors needed to preach subservience to the authorities ahead of time in preparation for the round-ups and to make it clear to the congregation that 'this is for their own good.' Pastors were told that they would be backed up by law enforcement in controlling uncooperative individuals and that they would even lead SWAT teams in attempting to quell resistance."

¹⁵"Is America Already a Police State?," Nathan Coe, *FreedomsPhoenix.com*, March 19, 2009.

¹⁶*Ibid.*

¹⁷In the spring of 2009, the GIVE (Generations Invigorating Volunteerism and Education) Act passed the U. S. House of Representatives (321-105) and the U. S. Senate (79-19), creating "mandatory volunteerism" by the young— which, of course, would potentially provide an opportunity for values and behavior modification by government-appointed supervisors, reminiscent of the Hitler Youth in Nazi Germany. Those who consider such a possibility far-fetched should ponder the words of presidential candidate Barack Obama during the 2008 campaign: "We cannot continue to rely on our military in order to achieve the national security objectives we've set. We've got to have a civilian national security force that is just as powerful, just as strong, just as well funded."

¹⁸According to a letter from Tom DeWeese of the American Policy Center

(June 2009), a proposed new international anti-gun treaty, the "Inter-American Convention Against Illicit Manufacturing of and Trafficking in Firearms, Ammunition, Explosives and Other Related Materials" (CIFTA), would overturn Second Amendment gun ownership rights. The U. S. would be required to adopt "strict licensing requirements" that supersede the Second Amendment—and, says Mr. DeWeese, "it is not too much of a stretch to include *assembling a firearm after cleaning* as 'illicit manufacturing' under the CIFTA treaty. That means guns could be confiscated if you don't have a federal license to clean or load [them]—with another license to buy ammunition for [them]."

[18]*The American Sentinel,* May 2009. The proposed legislation, the "Cybersecurity Act of 2009" (S. 773 and S. 778), would "give the White House sweeping new powers to access private on-line data, regulate the cybersecurity industry and even shut down Internet traffic in an 'emergency.' [The bills] would also grant the Secretary of Commerce access to all privately-owned information networks, '*without regard to any provision of law, regulation, rule, or policy restricting such access.*' In plain English, the feds are seeking the power to control how the Internet is used by private citizens. . . ."

[19]Kathy Lehman, "Ultimate Civil Liberties Threat! Americans to Become Serfs on the King's Estate," *The DeWeese Report* (April 2009), p. 10. The Food Modernization Act of 2009 (FSMA) "mandates registration of every 'food production facility,' which the bill defines as 'any farm, ranch, orchard, vineyard, aquaculture facility, or confined animal-feeding operation;' and every 'food establishment,' which the bill defines as 'a slaughterhouse . . . , factory, warehouse, or facility owned or operated by a person located in any State that processes food or a facility that holds, stores, or transports food or food ingredients.' The fine print of the FSMA will subject hobby gardeners, home canners, anyone with a few chickens, or anyone who 'holds, stores, or transports food'—including mushrooms or wild berries gathered in the wild—to registration, extensive management, and inspection by a huge new bureaucracy, the Food Safety Administration (FSA)—even if the food items will only be consumed personally."

[20]McAlvany, op.cit. p. 137. Particularly dangerous is EO12919, issued by President Clinton on June 6, 1994. Entitled "National Defense Industrial Resources Preparedness," this Executive Order "gives the president complete power to seize or allocate all public and private materials, services, facilities, food resources, food resource facilities, distribution of farm equipment and commercial fertilizer; construction materials, health resources, all forms of energy, and all forms of civilian transportation. Under this Executive Order, the president's National Security Council will be in charge of controlling and distributing ALL U. S. resources."

Other ominous Executive Orders would allow the government to mobilize civilians into work brigades (EO11000); take over all health, education, and welfare functions (EO11001); designate the Postmaster General to operate a national registration of all persons (EO11002); relocate communities, designate areas to be abandoned, and establish new locations for populations (EO11004);

and control all mechanisms of production and distribution, along with wages, salaries, credit, and the flow of money in U. S. financial institutions, while also stipulating that when a state of emergency is declared by the president, Congress cannot review his action for six months (EO11921).

[21]*Ibid.*, p. 78. Assets seized include cash, homes, cards, businesses, and property. Less than 10% of these seizures are drug-related; most of the victims are honest people who've unknowingly violated one or more of the countless number of government regulations now in effect.

[22] *Ibid.*, pp. 145-146. Under martial law (rule by the military), the Constitution (and the legal protections it gives to citizens) would be suspended. People suspected of a crime could be arrested and held indefinitely without trial; there would be no freedom of speech and no freedom of assembly, and the media would be subject to censorship.

An interesting—and indeed, frightening—observation on U. S. history and its current relevance is made by Gurudas, who states, "There was a broad repression of dissent during the Civil War. While Lincoln saved the Union, the general public and many historians have largely forgotten or have forgiven his repressive measures. A more balanced approach to his presidency would bring more criticism of his emergency actions that were often not necessary or legal under the Constitution. . . . On September 24, 1862 Lincoln declared martial law and suspended the writ of habeas corpus throughout the nation. . . . *There is no evidence that Lincoln's proclamation of martial law was ever lifted* [emphasis added]. . . . If martial law from the Civil War is still in place, as appears to be the case, this is a dagger pointing at the heart of the people. People should not be fooled into thinking that the continued existence of martial law could not be used to violate the Constitution" (Gurudas, *Teason: The New World Order*. pp. 178-180).

[23]McAlvany, op.cit. p. 55.

[24]Report by Bill Van Auken, quoted in "Is America Already a Police State?," Nation Coe, March 20, 2009. According to this same article, "Spencer S. Hsu and Ann Scott Tyson of *The Washington Post* report that 'the U. S. military expects to have 20,000 uniformed troops inside the United States by 2011' under the guise of assisting 'state and local officials [to] respond to a nuclear terrorist attack or other domestic catastrophe, according to Pentagon officials.'"

The article continues, "Even the elite are on edge. Former national security advisor Zbigniew Brzezinski has warned of riots within the United States. IMF Managing Director Dominiqu Strauss-Kahn has also warned of 'riots and unrest.' Naomi Wolf, author of *The End of America: Letters of Warning to a Young Patriot,* and *Give Me Liberty: A Handbook for American Revolutionaries,* has identified a series of key steps would-be dictators take to close down a more or less 'open' society, a blueprint for turning representative republics into outright fascist dictatorships. These steps were present in the development of every fascist state in modern history, and every society that displayed all of them eventually became a fascist dictatorship. *All are now present in America*" [emphasis added].

[25]Kelly Patricia O'Meara, "Deadly Force and Individual Rights," *Insight*, Nov. 8, 1999, p. 15. Local police officers are also capable of using intimidation and force against persons holding counter-cultural values (though innocent of any real crime). For instance, *Whistleblower* (Feb. 2009, p. 47) reports on a raid of a family-run food cooperative in LaGrange, Ohio, on December 1, 2008. Because the arrangement was limited to friends and neighbors, the family questioned the requirement that they obtain a license for their co-op. In response, law enforcement officials used "SWAT-style tactics," bursting into their home and holding family members—including children—at gunpoint, before confiscating their personal food supply.

[26]Gurudas, op.cit. (p. 195) writes, "On September 5, 1994, [Russian] General Pavel Grachev acknowledged that U. S. and Russian forces were conducting joint exercises in the U. S. as well as Russia to deal with riots, terrorist attacks, and other emergencies. . . . While the Pentagon claims that reports of Soviet-bloc equipment spotted in the U. S. are just old surplus, numerous photos shows that the latest Russian equipment is showing up all across the U. S. This includes the Russian Hind-E helicopter, SA-13 missile launcher, SA-13 Gopher surface-to-air missile system, BTR-60 armored personnel carrier, and T-72 and T-80 tanks. There are clearly too many Russian tanks and armor here to just be used in target practice and training exercises as the government claims, and none of this equipment is listed in the Pentagon inventory of military equipment".

[27]Bob Unruh, "Census GPS—Tagging Your Home's Front Door," *WorldNetDaily.com*, May 5, 2009. According to the article, there is "an army of some 140,000 workers hired in part with a $700 million taxpayer-funded contract to collect GPS readings for every front door in the nation. The data collection, presented as preparation for the 2010 Census, is pinpointing with computer accuracy the locations and has raised considerable concern from privacy advocates who have questioned why the information is needed."

[28]"FEMA Concentration Camps," http://www.sianews.com/modules. php?name =News&file_article&sid=1062.

[29]Gurudas, op.cit. pp. 199-200. More recently, Rep. Ron Paul of Texas stated during a 2006 interview that the Military Commission Act "officially allows for citizen concentration camp facilities" (*The DeWeese Report*, Jan. 2007, p. 6). Also a bill introduced in Congress in early 2009, the National Emergency Centers Act, or HR 645, authorized the DHS to create a network of FEMA camps. These are intended to house U. S. citizens during a national emergency; however, the bill also states that the camps would be available "to meet other appropriate needs, as determined by the Secretary of Homeland Security"—a mandate that could allow the forced detention of U. S. citizens under various circumstances (*prisonplanet.com*, Feb. 2, 2009).

Also, according to Kurt Nimmo in "Army National Guard Advertises for 'Internment Specialists" (*Infowars.com*, July 31, 2009), "Army Regulation 210-35, entitled 'Civilian Inmate Labor Program,' provides 'guidance for establishing and managing *civilian inmate labor programs* [emphasis added] on Army installations."

Chapter 14

What to Expect and What to Do

The theme of a future religious persecution appears in the writings of many Catholic saints and visionaries, including St. Hildegard (12th c.), Abbot Joachim Merlin (13th c.), Ven. Bartholomew Holzhauser (17th c.), Sr. Jeanne le Royer (18th c.), Bl. Anna-Katarina Emmerich and Bl. Anna-Maria Taigi (both 19th c.), and Sr. Natalia of Hungary (20th c.), among many others.

Some of these prophecies refer to the terrible suffering that will be inflicted upon the Church by the Antichrist near the end of time, but many seem to point to situations and events entirely separate from this final persecution. Particularly timely are the prophecies of Ven. Bartholomew Holzhauser, who warned that "heretics and tyrants will come suddenly and unexpectedly; they will break into the Church while bishops, prelates, and priests are asleep," and of Sr. Jeanne le Royer, who stated that "When the persecution against the Church has spread like a wild raging fire, *even to places where it was thought there was no danger* [emphasis added], then the Lord, Who knows how to draw glory out of everything, will suddenly command the mighty fire stream of Satan to halt. Then a universal peace will be proclaimed."

Our Lady has reportedly spoken of a present and coming time of persecution to Fr. Stefano Gobbi, founder of the Marian Movement of Priests.[1] Visionary John Leary claims to have received numerous messages from Jesus regarding a coming persecution of the Church here in the United States,[2] and in January 2009, a priest in Michigan was reportedly given a message by St. Therèse of Lisieux, who warned him, "In a short time, what took place in my native country [a reference to the religious persecution accompanying the French Revolution], will take place in yours. The persecution of the Church is imminent. Prepare yourself."

In the near future we may see government attempts to require the licensing not only of religiously-run institutions such as hospitals, orphanages, and nursing homes, but also of churches themselves, along with religious schools and other private groups and organizations. (This seems to be the desire of important elements within the United Nations and the U. S. government.[3]) Those religious groups which submit can be subjected to ever-growing restrictions later on; those groups and individuals who refuse can be immediately criminalized and repressed. Parental authority over children will likely be a crucial battleground; the idea that "it takes a village to raise a child" may come to mean that parents are judged inadequate to teach, discipline, and supervise their children without government licensing and control. (Indeed, turning children against their parents was a key element in Communism's persecution of religion in the Soviet Union.)

Any serious assault on the Church will likely involve the implementation of laws which Catholics will be unable to obey in good conscience. For instance, Catholic hospitals may be required to perform abortions and assisted suicide (and in fact, there have been such legislative attempts in the past[4]). The "equal rights for women" movement (which initially promoted some legitimate goals) may be twisted into a weapon to use against the Church, in which a refusal to ordain women as priests will be considered a violation of U. S. law. Similarly, the Church's refusal to recognize or perform same-sex "marriages" may be judged a violation of homosexuals' rights, resulting in lawsuits, civil penalties, and perhaps even criminal charges against bishops and priests.

We may see increasing efforts to attack Christianity's influence on American society; for example, opponents of religion may demand that we not "impose our values" on others. (Indeed, pro-abortion activists often mouth clichés using such specious reasoning.) Historical revisionism will likely play an important role in such efforts; churches may have to defend themselves against charges that they "supported slavery" and were "absent from the civil rights movement" (much as the Catholic Church, and particularly Pope Pius XII, is wrongly charged with silent complicity in the Nazi Holocaust[5]).

The Catholic Church, of course, will be a primary target of

such attacks; its unyielding opposition to artificial contraception will be blamed for much unnecessary poverty and suffering (even though the "overpopulation crisis" is a myth), and its rejection of *in vitro* fertilization, cloning, embryonic stem cell research, and similar experiments and discoveries will be portrayed as proof of its anti-scientific prejudice and unwillingness to accept modern realities.

Such vilification will also occur on an individual scale; we might reasonably expect many more false accusations of child molestation and sexual misconduct to be lodged against bishops, priests, and other parish ministers. (Needless to say, past failures on the part of Church leaders in America to address genuine cases of clerical sexual misconduct with young people will make these contrived charges much more credible.) Large segments of the media can be expected to cooperate quite willingly with this campaign of slander and negative publicity.

An additional factor involves the possibility of a schism—that is, the breaking away of part of the Church from the authority of the Pope. If the American Catholic Church separates from Rome, either formally or unofficially, it may be tempted to persecute (or acquiesce in the persecution of) those Catholics remaining faithful to the Holy Father. Enemies of the Church would be very happy to play off one group against the other, and because the children of this world are more skilled at such maneuvering than the children of God (cf. Lk. 16:8), in all likelihood faithful Catholics would have much to suffer.

There are certain things we might do to prepare ourselves in case a religious persecution is in fact coming to the United States. First, and most importantly, it's necessary to pray for guidance and discernment. Is all the information presented in these last few chapters truly an indication of what might come, or just a series of unrelated coincidences? Are those who fear or expect a religious persecution unduly pessimistic, or are they truly prophetic voices warning us of approaching danger? Is persecution inevitable, or is it still possible to avert it in some way? We cannot expect to discover the answers to these questions on our own; we need God's wisdom and guidance, for without His grace we may easily be misled. In all things, we must seek to know and act upon God's will, not our own.

Second, if we believe some form of danger lies ahead for the Church, we must maintain and even deepen our own relationship with Christ. Many Christian authors have written on the importance of building on a solid spiritual foundation in order to withstand the storms of persecution.[6] The Lord asks us to use times of relative peace to prepare for future possible danger; such preparation should include regular prayer, along with Scripture and other spiritual reading, and acts of penance. Just as soldiers train for battles that may or may not come, so should we prepare for possible challenges to our faith.

Third, we should become more knowledgeable about what's happening in the world and especially in our own country; we should make a deliberate effort to see the "big picture." Are new laws being proposed which could create problems for religious believers? Are current movies and TV shows becoming bolder in their attacks on the Faith? Are the latest technological advances threatening our privacy and freedom? Keeping informed on these and similar issues doesn't mean becoming paranoid, but we should remain vigilant and concerned—for Jesus calls upon us to stay awake and keep watch (cf. Mk. 13:37).

Fourth, instead of merely reacting to events, we should take a proactive stance by vigorously defending our religious freedom. This would include voting only for those candidates who respect and are willing to defend our Judeo-Christian heritage; contacting our elected representatives and public officials regarding the issues of the day; writing strong letters of protest to organizers or sponsors of entertainment or public events which mock or attack our Christian beliefs; using letters to the editor to defend the Church's teachings and values, and to educate the general public; and joining and supporting such organizations as the Catholic League, Focus on the Family, and the American Family Association.[7]

Fifth, it's worth considering joining and supporting one of the organizations helping Christians throughout the world who are already suffering persecution.[8] Our solidarity with those who are suffering for their faith is a way of expressing our unity in Christ (cf. Heb. 13:3), and quite possibly will prove spiritually beneficial as we prepare for our own challenges; after all, God is more likely to help persons who show concern for others.

Sixth, we should keep a proper perspective. A leader in the World Evangelical Fellowship made an important point: "The reasons Christians are being persecuted is because we are winning, not because we are losing."[9] Satan knows that his time is short, and that the victory promised through the Immaculate Heart of Mary draws near; therefore, we should see the frightened roars of his servants for what they are: the death rattles of a doomed and defeated kingdom.

Last, we should place our trust completely in God and refuse to give in to fear. Jesus has promised that if the time comes when we are on trial for our faith, we will be given the strength to stand firm and the words to say in response to our accusers (Lk. 12:11-12), and numerous persecuted Christians have testified that this is so.[10] Moreover, various contemporary private revelations suggest that if a persecution comes, many Christians will be led by their guardian angels to places of refuge.[11] The Lord will never abandon us, and nothing—not even persecution—can separate us from His love (Rm. 8:35).

Regarding the possibility of a religious persecution in America, the Lord asks us to be watchful and ready, to reject the temptation to be fearful, and to turn to Him in all our needs. Most of us are proud to be citizens of the United States, but our true allegiance is, and always should be, to the Kingdom of God. The blessings and freedoms we've experienced as Americans must not lessen our willingness to surrender everything to Christ, even to the point of dying in His Name—for in this way alone will we produce a rich harvest (cf. Jn. 12:24-25).

NOTES

[1]In an alleged locution of March 3, 1979, Our Lady stated that sometimes the Church "is persecuted in an open and violent manner; she is despoiled of everything and prevented from preaching the Gospel of Jesus. But in these times, the Church is often subjected to an even greater ordeal; she is persecuted in a subtle and painless manner, by being deprived bit by bit of the oxygen which she needs to live. Then an attempt is made to bring her to compromise

with the spirit of the world, which thus enters into her and affects and paralyzes her vitality. Collaboration is often brought about through a most subtle form of persecution; an outward show of respect for her has become the surest way to strike her. A new technique has been discovered by which she can be put to death with no outcry and without shedding blood."

Speaking to the priests, Our Lady continued, "The same hours of suffering that my Son Jesus lived through are awaiting you too, beloved sons: the hours of Gethsemane, when He experienced the interior agony of being abandoned, betrayed and denied by His own. . . . If this is the road trodden by the Master, it is also the road which you too much tread, you His faithful disciples, as the purification of the entire Church becomes more painful."

[2]For instance, in an alleged message of May 18, 1994, Jesus states, "I tell you, they will desecrate My churches even as has happened before. They will be made into museums and the like [and] My Presence will be profaned as the religious persecution begins." Also, on November 25, 1997, the visionary saw many churches with the steeples torn down; Our Lord explained, "My people, My Church will be persecuted as never before. Your churches will be desecrated and changed into museums or burned down. Only a few will be spared that are places of holy ground. When you see this persecution come, you will need to flee the cities to your underground churches."

[3]McAlvany, op.cit. p. 107. It should be remembered that the Nazis at first only registered the Jewish population of Germany; later this information was used to round up the Jews and ship them off to concentration camps and extermination centers.

[4]In the March 2000 issue of *HLI Reports* (published by Human Life International), Fr. Richard Welch wrote that "politicians, anti-life groups and the news media [in California] and in other states are plotting to compel Catholic hospitals to commit sterilizations, offer abortifacient contraceptives, give out 'morning after' abortifacients, abort babies, and make referrals for such grave sins, or else lose all taxpayer funding. . ." (p. 2). Furthermore, a California law which took effect January 1, 2000 orders all employer-paid health insurance plans to include contraceptives in their prescription drug coverage. According to Fr. Welch, the law's "conscience clause" is so weak that "it could force Catholic schools, social service agencies and hospitals to peddle contraceptives (which are mostly abortifacients) or violate 'the law.'" The California Catholic Conference has stated that this law in effect fails to grant Catholic organizations a conscience clause exception, thereby making it a "gross violation of our religious freedom. . . ."

[5]One example of such revisionist history, John Cornwell's *Hitler's Pope: The Secret History of Pius XII*, has been criticized by many reputable historians for its flawed scholarship and not-so-hidden agenda (and Cornwell himself later acknowledged a number of errors in his work). See, for instance, the review by Ronald J. Rychlak in the December 1999 issue of *Catalyst*, the newsletter of the Catholic League.

⁶In his book *More Than Conquerors*, Brother Andrew of Open Door Ministries (an inter-denominational group ministering to persecuted Christians) writes, "Whether or not an individual has learned to have real communication (prayer) with God may be the single most important factor in his surviving victoriously as a Christian" (as quoted in McAlvany, op.cit. p. 317). Pat Brooks writes in *A Call to War With Prayer Power*, "Fasting is the golden key that unlocks the life of victory for every overcomer who is sold out to Almighty God. . . . Anyone who longs for spiritual victory will, sooner or later, learn to fast" (McAlvany, op.cit. p. 335). Last Rev. Richard Wurmbrand (in *Preparing for the Underground Church*) relates the story of a pastor who had committed adultery, and warns, "His sin has not been what he has done on that evening; the circumstances were such that he could not resist the temptation. Rather that twenty years before, when not thus tempted, he had *not* said to himself, 'During my pastoral life different things will happen to me. Among other things it will happen that I will be tempted to sexual sin. I will not commit it then.' You have to prepare yourself beforehand for all eventualities. We have to prepare for suffering" (McAlvany, op.cit. p. 337).

⁷The Catholic League for Religious and Civil Rights can be contacted at 450 Seventh Avenue, New York, NY 10123; (212) 371-3191; or go to www.catholicleague.org. The AFA (American Family Association) can be reached at P. O. Drawer 2440, Tupelo, MS 38803; www.afa.net. Focus on the Family can be contacted at Focus on the Family (no street address needed), Colorado Springs, CO 80995; 1-800-232-6459; www.focusonthefamily.com.

⁸Two such organizations are the Voice of the Martyrs (P. O. Box 443, Bartlesville, OK 74005; 918-337-8015); and the Cardinal Kung Foundation (P. O. Box 8086, Ridgway Center, Stamford, CT 06905; 203-329-9712), an organization which supports the Underground Church in China.

⁹McAlvany, op.cit. p. 293.

¹⁰*Ibid.*, p. 307. McAlvany writes, "This author once asked the late Dimitru Dudman how he handled the fear when he knew he was going to be arrested or beaten by the Romanian secret police. He acknowledged that he had some fear prior to an arrest, but that when the event actually happened, that the Holy Spirit took his fear from him, gave him a supernatural peace, and also gave him the words to say."

¹¹Numerous messages of Jesus allegedly given to John Leary, for instance, state that while some members of the Church may be arrested during a persecution, they'll be given the grace to stand firm and to die as martyrs (immediately entering Heaven as a result). Most faithful Catholics, however, will be led by their angels in a timely manner to places of safety (eluding the surveillance of the authorities), where the Lord will provide for their spiritual and material needs.

Section E

Our Call to Heroism and Holiness

Chapter 15

True Love vs. Moral Blindness

During World War I, almost one million French and German soldiers were killed or wounded in a single battle in 1916: the Battle of Verdun. Near Verdun, in eastern France, there used to be a small village named Fleury; during the fighting, it was captured and recaptured again and again, changing hands eleven times. The town was completely destroyed, and was never rebuilt; it doesn't exist today. Instead, the area is an outdoor memorial, with historical markers indicating which buildings stood on a certain spot: the butcher's shop, the mayor's home, the tailor's shop, the schoolhouse, and so on. Only one building is to be found in Fleury today: a small memorial chapel, built after the war.

At times the French can be petty and vindictive. For example, while all the crosses in military cemeteries for French, British, and American soldiers (killed in either World War I or World War II) are painted white, the crosses in German military cemeteries on French soil are all painted brown. The Germans would like to paint the crosses of their soldiers white, too, but the French government won't allow it—for they believe the Germans, as invaders of France twice in the 20th century, don't deserve to be honored with a color signifying innocence or purity.

The French can be vindictive, but that didn't happen with the memorial in Fleury. The chapel there isn't named, as one might expect, "Notre Dame de Fleury" (Our Lady of Fleury), nor even "Notre Dame de France." Instead, it's named "Notre Dame de Europa"—"Our Lady of Europe." This site, where so much French blood was spilled, is set aside as a place of prayer and peace for the well-being of all Europe, not just France. This is a beautiful example of trying to see the larger picture: namely, that God loves all of us, and that our happiness and spiritual well-being comes from living in and sharing that love. Sometimes we as Americans and Catholics live up to that ideal; many times we fall short.

Back in 1998, two different sixth grade teachers were in the news: one as a hero, the other as a disgrace. Shannon Wright was a teacher who, along with four students, was shot and killed on a school playground in Arkansas during a tragic act of violence; she saved the life of a student by diving in front of the girl and taking that bullet that otherwise would have killed her. Mary Kay LeTourneau, on the other hand, was a teacher in Washington State who became lovers with one of her young students, bore his child, and later, after leaving her husband and children, had another baby with him. She claimed that the two of them "loved each other," but there's something very wrong with this so-called "love."

Shannon Wright's love was genuine, Christ-like, and of a type that didn't hurt anyone else; speaking of her sacrifice, her grieving husband said, "That's just the sort of thing Shannon would do for her students." Mary Kay LeTourneau's so-called love was selfish, misdirected, and very hurtful to others; her stunned husband and children couldn't understand why their wife and mother would abandon them and cause them such pain. There was a big difference in the motives and actions of those two teachers, but, unfortunately, not everyone understands or accepts that fact.

Our nation is increasingly afflicted by moral short-sightedness and spiritual myopia. No longer is there a widespread acceptance of objective truth, personal accountability, and ethical standards; much of our society seems to believe that anything can be acceptable if you're able to get away with it, and that determining "right" and "wrong" is just a matter of sufficiently twisting around your conscience so as to be comfortable with all your decisions and desires. (For example, when a well-known actor and producer was criticized some years ago for having a romantic relationship with his stepdaughter, he excused himself by saying, "The heart wants what the heart wants.")

An unwillingness to acknowledge unchanging moral standards creates a condition of spiritual blindness, and this leads to other types of blindness, or an inability to see and understand simple truths. (This, by the way, explains why people who are undecided on abortion, and even some who call themselves "pro-choice," find the issue of partial-birth abortion so uncomfortable and unsettling: it's too hard for them to deny to themselves that a child is being killed.) As Jesus said, "I came into this world for judgment, so that those who do not see might see, and those who do see might become blind" (Jn. 9:39). If we persistently reject the truth God reveals, we inevitably lose our ability to think and act rationally (as indicated by a number of problems in contemporary America[1]). Not only do we create more difficulties for ourselves in a worldly sense; we also subject ourselves to divine judgment—for as Scripture warns, "Woe to those who call evil good, and good evil, who change darkness into light, and light into darkness" (Is. 5:20).

America's moral eyesight has become very blurred, and as a result, our society accepts so many things that would have been vehemently rejected by most generations of Americans, including: the presence of rampant vulgarity, immorality, and disrespect for traditional values and authority in popular culture and entertainment, including prime-time television (and even during what used to be called TV's "family hour"); welfare dependency; declining educational standards; the categorization of certain types of destructive, anti-social behavior as "disabilities"; judicial arrogance, in which appointed judges set aside election results and manipulate the Constitution in accord with their own personal views; excessive regulation and bureaucratization, which penalizes hard work and risk-taking; a sense of entitlement, in which people expect society and particularly government to meet all their materials needs, instead of taking responsibility for themselves; a "bread and circuses" mentality which exalts excitement, entertainment, and personal comfort above everything else; and a widespread refusal to oppose blatantly immoral government policies and social values for fear of being thought "judgmental" or "politically incorrect."

These things would not have surprised St. Paul, for he recognized a link between wickedness and moral confusion. In 2nd Thessalonians he asked his converts to pray for him and his fellow missionaries, "that we may be delivered from perverse and wicked people, for not all have faith" (3:2), and in the Letter to the Romans he spoke of sinful pagans whose senseless minds were darkened after giving themselves over to disordered lusts: "Since they did not see fit to acknowledge God, He handed them over to the undiscerning mind to do what is improper" (1:28).

When a nation or people chooses to live in sin, wisdom inevitably vanishes, and the ability to see the "big picture"—the meaning of life, and the reality of death and judgment—disappears.

There's a saying that "in the land of the blind, the one-eyed man is king." That's the situation now facing committed Christians: though we may be "one-eyed" in the sense of not having a complete understanding of our times or in lacking the full moral clarity of saints and other extraordinary people, we are much more spiritually informed and prepared than perhaps a majority of the world's population. Possessing the truth is a great blessing, and a great responsibility. The Lord is calling upon us to see the big picture, to demonstrate our fidelity to Him, and to reflect His light in a world filled with darkness, using our influence and example to bear witness to the truth of the Gospel.

NOTES

[1]To cite just a few examples: It's long been recognized that terrorists would have an easy time sneaking small nuclear devices into the United States—but even so, since 9-11, relatively little has been done to gain control of our nation's borders; most serious efforts have been derailed by politics. Also, teachers' unions such as the NEA are among the most strident supporters of abortion—even though this support works against their own self-interest (for fewer children being born in America eventually means a smaller school-age population and a decreased need for teachers). The economy is staggering under the costs of ever-expanding government (both in absolute terms, and as a percentage of gross national product). Our political leaders, instead of making hard choices and cutting spending, continually add massively expensive new social programs and entitlements, further increasing the deficit and national debt (literally spending as if there were no tomorrow). Religion, because of its teaching of personal accountability to God, has always been an essential source

of moral values and good citizenship—but some of our nation's cultural elite are more determined than ever to remove every element of religious influence from our society (even though crime, illegitimacy, and other social pathologies have exploded over the past half-century). Future generations will look back at contemporary America and wonder how such a formerly great nation could have fallen so completely into a state of moral and societal insanity.

Chapter 16

Spiritual Guerilla Warfare

It often seems that we as Christians are swimming against the tide, and that it's all we can do just to hold onto our values in the face of the all the spiritual dangers we've been considering, including the changing values of our society, the ever-more intrusive role of technology, the prevalence of religious counterfeits, the very real possibility of a religious persecution in our country, and the moral blindness that afflicts so many of our fellow citizens.

Nevertheless, the Lord does not want us just to sit back passively and hope for the best; He expects us to be "salt for the earth" and "light for the world" (Mt. 5:13-16), so that our influence and example may inspire people to become more like Shannon Wright than Mary Kay LeTourneau, and may assist our society in overcoming its moral blindness, just as the French demonstrated a nobility of character in creating a memorial chapel at Fleury in honor of Our Lady of Europe.

We must be prepared for whatever may come, and while this may include some practical arrangements (such as storing food and other supplies in case of a possible future economic or even societal collapse), our spiritual preparations must take priority. This means, primarily, being in a state of grace, praying each day (particularly the Rosary), receiving the Sacraments regularly, and developing a strong sense of trust in God. Jesus is the Good Shepherd, and He will never leave the flock untended. If we're not yet completely confident of this fact, we need to begin praying each day for an increased spirit of trust and faith.

Our Lord expects us to use the opportunities we're given to bear witness to Him. It may appear the odds are against us, and the situation will probably seem even worse in the future. However, God has given us powerful spiritual weapons—an can be discussed in terms of what we might call "spiritual guerilla warfare." Guerillas, of course, are resistance fighters who are used to being outnumbered and out-gunned; rather than letting themselves be overwhelmed in a head-on fight, they choose their battles carefully.

In a spiritual sense, this is what Jesus was talking about when He called His followers to be as "shrewd as serpents and innocent as doves" (Mt. 10:16). It's unlikely any of us will have the opportunity to launch a direct attack against the forces of sin through a bold proclamation of the Gospel, whether by addressing Congress or the United Nations, having a heart-to-heart talk with the President, aiding in the miraculous conversion of a notorious sinner, writing a best-selling religious book, or anything else of a dramatic nature. Sometimes it's hard enough just to influence our own families and loved ones. No, God doesn't ask for miracles from us; He simply seeks genuine faith, lived out each day. For most of us, this is the means by which we can guide others to Jesus. We must do this, of course, not in a spirit of pride and self-righteousness, but one of humility and compassion.

Sometimes we can correct or influence other people by our gentle example. To give a personal example, I was once leading a Rosary in a funeral home, and the people—led by one gentleman in particular—were racing through their half of each Hail Mary. I could have turned around and said, "Please don't rush through the prayers," but that might have embarrassed someone. Instead, when they finished rattling off their part of the prayer, I waited in silence until we reached the point where I thought the Hail Mary should have ended, and only then did I begin the next one. It took three decades, but eventually the people realized they weren't saving any time by rushing through their part of each Hail Mary, so they slowed down and prayed more reverently—without my having to say anything directly.

This sort of "holy foot-dragging" or "sacred subversion," practiced patiently and gently, can influence the pace or direction of things so as to bring about a situation that's more pleasing to God. For instance, if the people around you learn that whenever they begin to gossip about someone, your automatic response will be, "Oh, that's too bad—let's say a prayer for him/her right now," you'll be able to help reduce the amount of gossiping occurring in the office or neighborhood—without getting involved in a confrontation, and without hurting anyone's feelings. Issuing a gentle challenge with a smile ("Come on, you know Jesus wouldn't want us to do that") is another way of preventing or short-circuiting a sinful situation. Our quiet, gentle, and loving adherence to our moral principles can end up having great influence over others.

Jesus wants us to do everything in a spirit of love, especially when it involves our enemies. Satan is counting on us responding to his servants in a spirit of fear, anger, and hatred, for this will end up increasing his power. If instead we respond with love, peace, and trust, the devil's plan is thwarted. Love breaks the circle of hatred. On Good Friday Jesus witnessed to this in the most wonderful and powerful way possible—and He desires that we bear witness to this truth, too.

I suspect one of the things that will surprise us when we get to Heaven is the discovery of how truly dangerous hatred and sin are, and of how infinitely much more powerful than they love is. In this regard, there are such spiritual realities as curses, spells, hexes, and other negative influences, and these can take on a life of their own, sometimes lasting for several generations or more.[1] They *always* end up hurting the people who use, utter, or initiate them, for the simple reason that we can never upset God's order of creation by doing evil without paying a painful price.[2] However, if we're the innocent targets, sometimes curses can also have a negative effect on us, even if we don't believe in them or are unaware of what's happening. The only defense is to follow Jesus' command to "Love your enemies, pray for those who persecute you" (Mt. 5:44).

When we love others in Christ's Name, especially persons who may be trying to hurt us, we limit their ability to do us any lasting spiritual harm. Love becomes something like a spiritual mirror, reflecting any negative energy back to its source. Now, our attitude can't be, "I'm going to love my enemies, so that if they try anything against me, they'll only be doing it to themselves; that'll fix their wagon." This sort of thinking means we're playing on the enemy's terms, in which case we'll lose.

No, we should strive to love everyone, without exception and without conditions; doing this unleashes great spiritual power and covers us with God's grace and protection. The more we love, the less we have to fear. Creating this sort of "love shield" is simply a matter of deliberately deciding that we love everyone, that we forgive all our enemies (known and unknown), and that we want everyone to be saved and to be blessed. (It's possible for us to do this even on behalf of people we don't like or respect, because this sort of love isn't a feeling we may or may not have; rather, it's a conscious choice we freely make.)

We can spiritually protect ourselves from people who hate us and who may seek to do us spiritual harm simply by loving them, and, of course, by remaining in a state of grace, receiving the Sacraments regularly, and by frequently praying for God's guidance and protection.

It's also necessary to be on guard against evil spirits. The devil is a reality; he seeks to harm us and deceive us, with the ultimate goal of dragging us down to his kingdom of hell (*Catechism*, par. 391-395). Even if he judges that—because of our love of God—there's little chance he'll be able to lead us to damnation, he continues working against us for two reasons: first, he hates us, and wants to inflict as much suffering on us as possible; and second, he hopes to minimize or eliminate our positive influence on others and on the world, thereby decreasing the glory we give to God while making his own efforts to ensnare people in sin more likely to succeed.

We don't have to limit ourselves to guarding against Satan's attacks; we can also fight back.[3] Some of the means are obvious: praying each day, reading the Bible, attending Mass and receiving Holy Communion and Confession regularly, spending time in Eucharistic Adoration, learning more about our Faith, promoting and defending the truths of Catholicism, associating with other people of strong faith and morals, giving a good example to others, helping others in need, faithfully fulfilling our duties in life without grumbling or complaining, offering up our sufferings and struggles as a sacrifice for the conversion of sinners, practicing the spiritual and corporal works of mercy,[4] accepting every opportunity life presents to act with patience and humility, and striving to overcome our faults and to grow in virtue. In addition to these necessary and valuable steps, however, there's also a form of spiritual warfare called the binding of spirits.

St. Mark's Gospel tells us that Jesus gave His followers authority over evil spirits (16:17). Using this authority isn't necessarily the same thing as a full-fledged exorcism, which only authorized priests may perform; in the context of spiritual warfare, the binding of spirits is a form of prayer available to all believers.[5] Binding evil spirits doesn't attempt to remove them or drive them away (as is the case in an exorcism), but merely prevents them from using their power on us or someone else.

A binding prayer merely requires us to say, in a whisper or soft voice, "Evil spirit, I bind you in the Name of the Lord Jesus Christ." (If we know or suspect the name of a specific spirit, we can address it that way: "Spirit of fear . . . spirit of lust . . . spirit of rebellion . . . spirit of deception," and so on.) Because the Name of Jesus is all-powerful, this removes the devil's ability to do us any immediate harm. (Similarly, whenever we feel or suspect any sort of negative spiritual influences, we might also say a Hail Mary or the Prayer to St. Michael the Archangel, or pray for the assistance of our guardian angel, St. Joseph, our patron saint, or any saint of our choice.)

It's frequently possible that we're being tempted or confused or deceived or agitated by Satan's spiritual agents without our realizing it. Obviously, it wouldn't be correct to blame everything on the devil, but he may be trying to influence more than we realize. Binding him in Christ's Name can stop him in his tracks. If we see someone else who may unknowingly be struggling with evil—perhaps an irritated or irritating family member or co-worker, a restless fellow parishioner at a prayer meeting, or a disturbed or upset stranger on the street or in the shopping mall—we can use the binding prayer in this situation. Saying it softly spares us from embarrassment if there isn't any evil influence at work, and protects us and the other person if the devil is indeed present and active.

In basketball there's a play called a "pick," in which one player runs interference for a teammate, getting in the way of an opponent so the teammate is free to drive to the basket or take a shot. That's what we're talking about in a spiritual sense: blocking possible evil influences through a binding prayer, so tha will be able hear God's call or proceed with his or her moral and religious duties free of demonic harassment.

We can do this for people known to or encountered by us personally, and also for people we've never met—especially those with heavy responsibilities. It's reasonable to assume, for instance, that the Pope and the President, because of their importance and influence, receive a lot of attention from the devil. We can help protect them by praying something like, "All evil spirits in the presence of the Holy Father or the President of the United States, I bind you in the Name of the Lord Jesus Christ." We might also pray that way for certain groups of people, such as criminals, gang members, abortionists, drug pushers, pornographers, pedophiles, and also for any public figures who seem to be living contrary to God's Will. Even if our prayers don't lead to someone's conversion, they may still limit the person's spiritual influence on others and reduce the amount of evil he or she is able to do.

We need to be aware of what's happening in the world and in our country, and also in the Church; just as importantly, when things aren't as they should be, we need to thwart our adversaries with love. Prayer—especially in front of the Blessed Sacrament—is very powerful; offering a Holy Hour for someone, or just a short period of prayer if that's all we have time for, can have unexpected and even miraculous results.

When we unlock the power of divine love and grace, allowing them to work within us, wonderful things can be accomplished, or unfortunate things can be prevented or delayed. The idea isn't to bring sinful people to tears of frustration, but to tears of repentance; we're not trying to mess with our opponents, but to bathe them in love, genuinely desiring their spiritual well-being. The more we love, the more we'll be able to accomplish for Jesus; the more we trust in Him, the more we'll be able to serve Him as an instrument of grace.

Our Lord once spoke of an exorcised demon returning to its earlier victim, finding the soul empty, and moving back in with seven even worse spirits (Lk.11:24-26). His point was that it's not enough just to be opposed to evil; it's also necessary to seek out and actively choose and promote what's good.

In terms of family life, this includes finding and providing good, wholesome entertainment and activities for children, teens, and adults. Instead of automatically turning on the TV, for instance, television shows should be selected with care; many times using the VCR to watch family-friendly movies and inspirational religious videos is a safer choice.

Another healthy form of entertainment is religious reading—in particular, good Christian fiction; it's a wonderful thing to read enjoyable books that reaffirm your faith while also stretching your imagination. Reading in general is very important as a way of staying informed about current events and learning more about Catholicism; faithful Catholic magazines and newspapers, and books from reliably orthodox publishers, should be present in every Catholic home. (Interesting and attractive Catholic books and magazines can also make wonderful gifts—especially to fallen-away Catholics or to persons searching for spiritual meaning in life.)

Besides all this, it's advisable to be involved in worthwhile parish activities and community events, and to share friendship and support with like-minded Christians. All these things will not only help us preserve our faith in a hostile culture, but also multiply our influence and allow the Holy Spirit to use us more effectively as agents of grace and signs of divine truth.

NOTES

[1]For a good, introductory discussion of this point, see *A Guide to Healing the Family Tree*, by Dr. Kenneth McAll (Queenship Publishing Company, 1996).

[2]Fr. José Antonio Fortea, *Interview With An Exorcist* (Ascension Press, 2006), pp. 110-112.

[3]Recommended books on the subject of spiritual warfare include *Angels & Devils*, by Joan Carroll Cruz (TAN Books and Publishers, 1999); *The Deceiver: Our Daily Struggle With Satan*, by Livio Fanzaga (Roman Catholic Books, 2000); and *An Arrow in His Hand*, by Maria Vadia (Queenship Publishing Company, 2006).

[4]The corporal (bodily or material) works of mercy are feeding the hungry, giving drink to the thirsty, clothing the naked, providing shelter to the homeless, visiting the sick and imprisoned, ransoming captives, and burying the

dead.

The spiritual works of mercy are instructing the ignorant, correcting sinners, advising the doubtful, showing patience to sinners and persons in error, forgiving others, comforting the afflicted, and praying for the dead.

[5]Benedict Herron OSB, *I Saw Satan Fall: The Ways of Spiritual Warfare* (New Life Publishing, 1997), p. 70.

Chapter 17

Happiness and Growth While Under Siege

We're in a spiritual and cultural war, and one of the key factors in any war is morale. Do we expect to win, or do we expect to lose? Many times our expectations will affect the outcome; therefore, it's important that each one of us develop our own personal attitude of joy, optimism, and hope. Not only will this outlook attract others, but it will also help us be more alert for opportunities to serve God and better prepared for His coming victory.

Our side *is* going to win; Jesus has guaranteed it—and that's a reason for rejoicing. The 1st Letter of St. Peter says, "Always be ready to give an explanation to anyone who asks you for a reason for your hope" (3:15). Having a certain cheerfulness or joyful spirit can prompt questions from others, and provide us with opportunities for witnessing; when someone asks, "Why are you always so happy?," it's a chance to respond, "Because of my relationship with Jesus," or "Because I'm so aware of and thankful for God's blessings," or "Because of what the Lord is doing in my life."

Some of the saints had a reputation for cheerfulness and even a good sense of humor, including St. Teresa of Avila, St. Thomas More, and St. Philip Neri, and this joyfulness was expressed even in the face of great trials. The English martyr Sir Thomas More, for instance, made a little joke with his executioner. While stepping up to the platform where he was about to be beheaded, More said, "Assist me up, if you please; coming down I can shift for myself." That sort of humor is a great expression of faith.

Our example truly can attract and inspire other people. Also, gentle humor can defuse tense situations, give us a reputation as down-to-earth people, make it easier for others to approach us and ask religious questions, and protect us from accusations that we're zealots, fanatics, or old fogeys. Humor can help us keep our perspective on things. Life's lessons are often a bitter pill; sometimes humor is the sugar-coating that helps them go down more easily.

In talking about spiritual growth, especially under challenging circumstances, the most important subject is obviously that of praying. We are called to pray always (cf. Lk. 18:1); this means forming the habit of responding to our opportunities. For instance: When driving past a Catholic church, we might silently pray to Christ in the tabernacle, "O Eucharistic Lord, I adore You." If we see a funeral procession, we can pray, "May this person rest in peace." When we hear a siren from a police car, fire truck, or ambulance, we can intercede, "Lord, bless and protect those who are in danger." When we learn of tragedies via the newspaper, TV, or radio, we can respond, "Dear God, please help and sustain all who suffer." If we see children on a playground, we can pray, "Lord Jesus, may these children always be happy and faithful to You." When driving past a hospital or nursing home, we might say, "O Lord, please bless all the residents or patients there and those who care for them." When sending off our children to school or our spouse to work—or, in fact, upon seeing anyone anywhere—we can pray silently or aloud, "I bless you in the Name of the Lord Jesus Christ."

We often underestimate the power of prayer, but the Letter of St. James says, "The fervent prayer of a righteous person is very powerful" (5:16). If all the Christians in our country prayed much more regularly—several times throughout the day, in addition to using spontaneous opportunities—our society would be transformed overnight. A tidal wave of grace would be released, the power of evil would shrink dramatically, and many of our country's problems would be lessened or completely washed away. I fear that when future Church historians look back upon our era, they'll wonder how we as Christians could have allowed society's values and moral standards to deteriorate so badly; if they were to come up with a concise explanation, I think it would be this: "They didn't pray nearly enough." This is one of our faults—and it's within our power to change it.

Evil is a negative force: it has no creative power of its own, and can only thrive and grow stronger in the absence of good. Many Christians have been remiss in their responsibilities toward God, the Church, and America; we haven't been leaven in our society, using our spiritual and moral influence as much as we should—and evil forces have moved into the vacuum. Our nation's destiny has been hijacked—but it doesn't have to be that way or stay that way. Good is stronger than evil, and if the forces of love and faith come together, cooperate, and exercise their spiritual power, evil will be forced to retreat. What we need is a second American Revolution—a spiritual and moral one.

Prayer is powerful—and the most powerful prayer of all is the Mass. An alleged message of Our Lady states, "Mass is the greatest prayer before God. You will never be able to understand its greatness."[1] Actively participating in Mass is the best possible use of our time. Not only are we preparing for eternity, but we can also make a difference here and now; not only are we personally growing in grace, but we can also offer our attendance at Mass, and our worthy reception of Holy Communion, as a powerful prayer on behalf of someone else. Each Mass has its stated intention, but it's also possible for everyone attending to have one or more personal intentions, too. The Mass makes present once again Jesus' one, perfect Sacrifice, and this Sacrifice has infinite value—so we shouldn't hesitate to offer our attendance at Mass for everyone and everything in need of our prayers, including our country and the Universal Church.

After the Mass itself, the most powerful prayer is the Rosary. Our Lady is supposed to have revealed, "I will bind Satan in chains made up of the thousands of Rosaries said by my children," and Sister Lucy of Fatima, in her 1957 interview with Fr. Augustine Fuentes, stated,

> The Most Holy Virgin in these last times in which we live has given a new efficacy to the recitation of the Holy Rosary. She has given this efficacy to such an extent that there is no problem, no matter how difficult it is, whether temporal or above all, spiritual, in the personal life of each one of us, of our families, of the families of the world, or of the religious

communities, or even of the life of peoples and nations, that cannot be solved by the Rosary.[2]

This form of prayer is a particularly powerful weapon against evil. For example, Fr. Gabriele Amorth, chief exorcist of the Vatican, observed, "One day a colleague of mine heard the devil say during an exorcism: 'Every Hail Mary is like a blow on my head. If Christians knew how powerful the Rosary was, it would be my end.'"[3]

Every time we say the Rosary, we're robbing the devil of a little bit more of his strength to do evil; we're part of the Church's counterattack against the kingdom of hell. The Rosary is also a very strong prayer on behalf of our families, a way of helping to confirm them in their faith and safeguard them from spiritual danger. This can be especially important when it comes to family members who no longer practice their faith.

You may have already learned that in such situations, the direct approach doesn't always work very well: when your family members stop going to church, challenging or nagging them on this may only push them farther away. The same thing can be true if your grown children are cohabiting, or engaged in other sinful activity. In this case, it's especially important to be as clever as serpents while remaining as innocent as doves.

This means, at the outset, making your position clear: while you'll always love your wayward family members, you don't approve of their actions or lifestyle. Once this point has been made in a firm and loving way, don't keep harping on it; instead, it's time to act in a subtle manner. This means, first of all, praying the Rosary for them. If you think it's possible your loved ones are being tempted or influenced by evil spirits, use a binding prayer whenever you can. If you have an adventurous spirit, you might sneak some holy water into their homes and sprinkle it around when no one is looking; you might also hide small blessed religious objects in the home, or give them a blessed religious item as a gift—perhaps a Bible, or a painting or statue of Jesus or Mary. At the same time, you can offer up every Mass you attend, and every Holy Communion you receive, as a spiritual gift or prayer on their behalf; you might even have a Mass offered for your special intention: namely, your loved ones' return to the Church.

Because of the difficult times in which we live, it's important that not only we ourselves be spiritually prepared, but that we assist as many other people as possible in doing this—particularly our own family members. Knowing that we're doing what Our Lord wants us to do will be a source of great peace, consolation, and even joy in the challenging days that are most likely coming, and our attitude of joyful hope—even as many other people are gripped by worry, confusion, and panic—may allow us additional opportunities to share the Good News of salvation in Jesus.

In some ways it's becoming more difficult to be a committed Christian than ever before. Therefore, we have to be as clever as serpents, staying abreast of what's happening in the world and in the Church, thinking ahead just in case things don't turn out quite the way we hope, and looking for opportunities to use our talents, abilities, and resources. At the same time we have to be as innocent as doves, trusting in Jesus, letting His Spirit guide us, and loving everyone we meet without exception.

This is our mission from Heaven. Not only is it *not* impossible; it's absolutely *essential*. Faith and love will see us through; they will help us recognize and understand the big picture, making sense of what's happening and allowing us to respond to everything, no matter how unexpected, in a spirit of trust and hope. Jesus is with us always, and He has guaranteed us the victory. As long as we keep this in mind, nothing else will ultimately matter; as long as we place all our hope in Jesus alone, we need not fear.

NOTES

[1]Michael H. Brown, *After Life: What It's Like in Heaven, Hell, and Purgatory* (Queenship Publishing Company, 1997), p. 70.

[2]Mark Fellows, *Sister Lucia: Apostle of Mary's Immaculate Heart* (Immaculate Heart Publications, 2007), p. 267.

[3]*Echo of Mary, Queen of Peace*, March-April 2003.

Chapter 18

Weapons in
Our Spiritual Arsenal

S t. John Bosco had a famous dream, in which a ship repre-
senting the Church was undergoing a fierce attack by its
enemies; however, the Bark of Peter was able to find safety
by anchoring itself to two immense columns which rose majesti-
cally out of the sea. The greater of the two held aloft a huge Host,
and on the base of the column were inscribed the words *"Salus
Credentium"*—"Salvation of the Faithful." The second, smaller
column held aloft a statue of the Immaculate Virgin Mary, with
an inscription on the base, *"Auxilium Christianorum"*—"Help of
Christians."[1] The holy 19th century Italian priest interpreted his
dream as meaning that the Eucharist and devotion to Mary would
be the two most important sources of spiritual strength and protection for Catholics during the trials and persecutions awaiting the
Church in the future.

The preceding chapter has spoken of the great value and importance of the Eucharist—specifically, attending Mass and worthily
receiving Holy Communion—and of devotion to Mary, especially
through the Rosary. These two sources of grace, more than any
others, will help us resist the siren calls and snares of this world,
and even give us the strength and courage to launch our own small
but valuable counterattacks within our own sphere of influence,
thus helping pave the way for the coming victory of the Immaculate Heart of Mary. Jesus promises, "Whoever eats My flesh and
drinks My blood has eternal life" (Jn. 6:54), and so the Eucharist
will preserve us from spiritual death—even if the world around us
is careening down the path to self-destruction. At the same time,
Our Lady's maternal intercession is very powerful with her Son

(cf. Jn. 2:1-11), and for this reason, the Rosary can be a source of innumerable blessings.

Those who have recourse to the Eucharistic Lord and to the Queen of Heaven will never be overcome by this world, but will share in the triumph of the two Hearts of Jesus and Mary. In addition to the Eucharist and the Rosary, the Church offers her children various other spiritual weapons, each of which can be extremely useful. Many Catholics are unaware of their power, yet the need for them is perhaps greater than ever before—and so this valuable and important list is offered here:

Eucharistic Adoration

In addition to receiving the actual Body and Blood of Christ in Holy Communion, we as Catholics are privileged to be able to pray and worship in the Real Presence of Jesus. We can do this, of course, by praying to Jesus in the tabernacle each time we come to church; we are especially blessed to be in church if and when Eucharistic Adoration takes place, with the actual Body of Christ exposed in the monstrance on the altar. There is no better setting for prayer, for pouring out our hearts to Jesus (sharing our sorrows and fears, our hopes and needs, our joys and thanks), and for interceding on behalf of others. Coming into a quiet church—whether for an hour or more, or just a few minutes—and worshipping the Eucharistic Lord is a wonderful way of setting aside our worries and burdens, spiritually "inoculating" ourselves from the false values and influences of society, and allowing divine grace to work ever more deeply within us. Those who regularly visit Jesus in church—especially during Eucharistic Adoration—become much more capable of resisting temptation, growing in virtue, and achieving an inner peace this world cannot give. To a large degree, this truth cannot be explained or verified, but must be personally experienced—and those who make a point of doing so will be well-equipped to face whatever challenges the future may hold.

Reconciliation (Confession)

A mother and her teenage son once came to me seeking help for an upsetting problem: some malign spiritual presence in their home was harassing them and making them feel very threatened.

What made the situation unusual was that the other two members of the family, the husband and teenage daughter, were completely unaffected. It happened that both the mother and son, unlike the others, were in a state of mortal sin; once I heard their confessions and absolved them, the sinister hold over them was broken, and they were no longer upset or disturbed.

The Sacrament of Reconciliation (also known as Confession or Penance) has great spiritual power, a power directly entrusted by Christ to His Church (cf. Mt. 16:19; Jn. 20:23)—and as such, it is always (after Baptism itself) the first step in breaking the hold of sin over a person's life. According to the *Catechism*, through this Sacrament "the sinner is healed and re-established in ecclesial communion" (par. 1448)—and thus strengthened for the ongoing spiritual struggle against the world, the flesh, and the devil. Partly because of our society's overemphasis on individual autonomy and its aversion to personal accountability (and also due, in some cases, to an earlier unpleasant experience in the confessional), many Catholics find this Sacrament difficult or extremely uncomfortable. Precisely because the act of humbly acknowledging one's sins and seeking forgiveness is so counter-cultural, however, it can be argued Catholics need Reconciliation perhaps more than ever before; certainly those who make use of the Sacrament will have a much easier time withstanding temptation and fulfilling God's plan for their lives. In today's morally deluded and corrupted world, Catholics who ignore or neglect the Sacrament of Reconciliation place themselves in grave and unnecessary spiritual peril. (A simple instruction on "How to Go to Confession" is given in Appendix A.)

Scripture and Spiritual Reading

One of the Psalms addresses the Lord by saying, "A lamp to my feet is Your word, a light to my path" (Ps. 119:105). God's Word in Sacred Scripture is indeed a source of spiritual light and an essential guide for us on our pilgrimage through life. Only through regular reading of the Bible can we truly hope to know our Savior, for, as St. Jerome asserted, "Ignorance of the Scriptures is ignorance of Christ." The Church, through which the Bible has come down to us, urges Catholics to read Scripture frequently (*Catechism*, par.

133), for God's Word is a "wellspring of prayer" (par. 2653) and a source of nourishment for Christian life (par. 141). Our world is constantly promoting the latest fads and offering us questionable benefits of passing value. Scripture, however, offers us eternal truths ordered to our salvation; therefore, no one firmly rooted in Sacred Scripture and Tradition is in danger of being led astray.

In addition, regular spiritual reading from reliable and approved Catholic sources is also of great value. According to St. Athanasius of Alexandria, "You will not see anyone who is truly striving after his spiritual advancement who is not given to spiritual reading." Such reading can be immensely valuable not only as a means of wisdom and enlightenment, but also as a source of grace and spiritual peace—for just as, in the words of St. Vincent de Paul, "you speak to God when at prayer, God speaks to you when you read." Satan desires to keep us so busy with unimportant things that we never "have time" for what truly matters. A regular period of Scriptural and spiritual reading (preferably each day) will help us avoid his snares and allow us to reflect God's light in a world darkened by sin.

Fasting and Penance

According to St. Robert Bellarmine, "The chief end of fasting is mortification of the flesh, so that the spirit may be strengthened more." In this regard, fasting can be a powerful form of penance, spiritual growth, and intercession (on behalf of oneself and others, including the larger community); moreover, it's also a powerful weapon against evil,[2] as it helps undermine Satan's kingdom and decreases his ability to tempt and deceive us. Modern medicine has recognized the physical benefits of fasting, and according to Mother Nadine of the Intercessors of the Lamb, "The Lord showed me that the cleansing and energizing that happens within our bodies during fasting, works the same way in the Mystical Body of Christ. Our fasting carries the cleansing power, the deliverance power to cast out the poison in His Mystical Body, the Church."[3]

There are different types of fasting: eating one less meal on a given day, taking only bread and water on certain days (such as Wednesdays and Fridays, as suggested in one alleged message of Our Lady), skipping dessert, giving up a food we enjoy, not eating between meals, eating less at each meal, etc. There are two important points to keep in mind: first of all, we must recognize our physical limitations, and not endanger our health or negatively affect our ability to perform our duties[4] (and medical guidance may be called for in this regard); second, Scripture warns us that even rigorous fasting isn't pleasing to God unless we are fulfilling our more important duty of showing compassion to others in His Name (cf. Is. 58:3-11). Assuming that our fasting is genuine and not for outward show (cf. Mt. 6:16; Lk. 18:12), it will be of great spiritual value to us (in part because of its counter-cultural nature in our hedonistic society). The same thing can be true of other acts of penance (getting up early in order to pray, turning off the TV in order to spend quiet time with the Lord, keeping silent whenever we're tempted to grumble or complain, etc.). Every act of penance we offer for God's glory, no matter how small, can discipline our wills, prepare us to face future spiritual challenges successfully, and give glory to God's Name. The word "sacrifice" comes from the Latin expression "to make holy" (*sacrum facere*)—and a sacrificial spirit is indeed a reliable path to holiness.

Devotion to Mary, the Angels, and the Saints

All the saints successfully overcame worldly temptations, allurements, and obstacles, and so it makes sense for us to imitate their virtues and seek their intercession and assistance. This is especially the case with the Virgin Mary, the Mother of God and the greatest of all the saints. As St. Bonaventure noted, "The gates of Heaven will open to all who confide in the protection of Mary," and according to St. John Berchmans, "If I love Mary, I am certain of perseverance, and shall obtain whatever I wish from God." In addition to regularly praying the Rosary, we can honor Our Lady through Perpetual Help devotions, making the Five First Saturdays,[5] entrusting ourselves to her Immaculate Heart,[6] and using any of the many different novenas, litanies, and other prayers and devotions offered by the Church in her honor. As our heavenly Mother, she is eager to help us grow ever closer to her Son Jesus—and as "Heaven's Treasurer," through whom all graces are dispensed, her intercession and spiritual protection are immensely powerful.

It's also spiritually profitable to cultivate a devotion to St. Joseph, our patron saints, and any other saints to whom we have an attraction—and in regard to the saints in the Church's liturgical calendar, it's useful to remember that the intercession of each saint can be especially powerful and fruitful on his or her own feast day. Additionally, we should frequently request guidance, assistance, and protection against temptations and every form of evil from our guardian angels and St. Michael the Archangel; as Scripture says, "For to His angels [the Lord] has given command about you, that they guard you in all your ways" (Ps. 91:11). It is not God's will that we struggle alone against evil; His saints and angels are eager to help us, and we are very wise if we seek their assistance.

The Divine Mercy Chaplet

In the 1930s, St. Faustina Kowalska, a Polish nun, was the recipient of many messages from Jesus, in which He stressed His infinite mercy and His ardent desire that sinners turn back to Him in a spirit of humility and trust. One of the devotions Our Lord taught Sr. Faustina was the Chaplet of Divine Mercy, a set of prayers to be recited on ordinary Rosary beads.[7] Jesus promised that "Even the most hardened sinner, if he recites this chaplet even once, will receive grace from My infinite mercy,"[8] and that by means of the Chaplet "you can ask and obtain anything, if what you ask for will be compatible with My Will."[9] While the Chaplet can be prayed, alone or with others, at any time, the ideal time is at 3pm, the Hour of Great Mercy (for it was at that hour that Jesus died on the Cross). Along with the other aspects of the Divine Mercy devotion (Divine Mercy Sunday, the Great Novena of Mercy, and the Image of Divine Mercy)—all of which have received official Church approval—the Chaplet of Divine Mercy was apparently reserved by Jesus until the 20th century, when the Message of Mercy would be needed more than ever before . . . and now that we've entered the 21st century, the need for and value of this great devotion continues to grow.

The Sign of the Cross

As Catholics, we automatically make the Sign of the Cross in many different situations. We may even take it for granted—but as one author notes, this gesture "is a powerful prayer. Through it, Satan is confronted with the reality that he has been vanquished."[10] There are many stories from the lives of the saints about its efficacy in overcoming demonic harassment (a method used successfully by St. Martin de Porres, St. Rita of Cascia, and St. Alphonsus Liguori, among others),[11] and it can also help us resist temptation and maintain a prayerful, recollected spirit. In fact, whenever we are about to undertake any project, type of work, or even leisure activity, we can begin with the Sign of the Cross—thereby honoring God and asking His blessing upon our efforts.

The Scapular

A scapular consists of two small rectangular pieces of cloth, attached by two strings; it is worn around the neck (with one piece of cloth on the breast and the other on the back), usually beneath one's clothes. Scapulars come in many different colors (red, green, white, and blue, etc.), but the most popular and common are brown scapulars, for very important graces are associated with them. On July 16, 1251, Our Lady of Mt. Carmel appeared to St. Simon Stock, a member of the Carmelite Order, and gave him the brown scapular, promising, "Whoever dies clothed with this holy scapular shall not suffer eternal fire." Those who are formally enrolled in the Order of the Scapular (a ritual which any priest may perform) may also share in what has come to be called the "Sabbatine Privilege." This means that for those who (1) wear the brown scapular, (2) observe chastity according to their state in life, and (3) pray the Rosary each day, Our Lady promises that if they are sent to be cleansed of their sins in purgatory after dying, she will personally release them and escort them into Heaven on the first Saturday after their death. Needless to say, this is an immensely valuable spiritual benefit offered by the Mother of God.

Medals

Religious medals portray Jesus, Mary, or one of the saints, and are "intended to excite devotion and prayer, and in general to signify the Christian's commitment to a holy life. . . ."[12] One of the most famous is based on an apparition of Our Lady to St. Catherine Labouré in 1830, in which Mary asked for a medal to be created in honor of her Immaculate Conception, promising, "Au. who wear it will receive great graces." So many amazing cures and conversions occurred following its creation and distribution that it became known as the "Miraculous Medal." Another important example is that of the St. Benedict Medal, which is considered "a formidable weapon against the evil spirits and a mighty help in keeping pure, in bringing about conversions and in guarding against contagious diseases."[13] These and other religious medals, when blessed by a priest, can—if worn or carried with genuine devotion by the owner—be a great source of grace and spiritual protection.

Holy Water and Other Sacramentals

Holy water (that is, water blessed by a priest) is not only a reminder of Baptism, but also a source of grace and spiritual protection—and as such, should be used frequently. Most parishes have provisions for people to take holy water home, and once there, it can be replenished very easily: simply add regular (unblessed) water to the partially empty holy water bottle or container, and as long as the amount added is less than the holy water remaining, all the water is thereupon blessed. This water can be used to bless persons, rooms, religious articles, and even non-religious items (such as pets, clothing, tools, and, if desired, food). Parents are also well-advised to bless their children's bedrooms on a regular basis (as a protection against nightmares and real or imagined demonic presence). Whenever a room or place has an unexplained sinister or uncomfortable feel to it, it should be thoroughly blessed with holy water—just in case evil spirits are actually present. St. Teresa of Avila tells us, "From long experience I have learned that there is nothing like holy water to put devils to flight and prevent them from coming back again."[14]

Sacramentals, according to the *Catechism*, are "sacred signs which bear a resemblance to the sacraments. They signify effects, particularly of a spiritual nature, which are obtained through the intercession of the Church" (par. 1667). There are various other sacramentals in addition to the ones already mentioned, including blessed salt, blessed oil, candles, crucifixes, holy cards, pictures or statues of Jesus and Mary, and other sacred objects. Our Lady, ac-

he alleged message, has advised us to protect ourselves
attack by keeping such blessed items with us[15]—and
spiritually dangerous times, such advice should be taken
very seriously.

Conclusion

Thus, the Church offers us many different spiritual weapons and defenses to use in our ongoing struggle against sin, temptation, and the unavoidable reality of evil in the world. Our affluent, arrogant, and technologically advanced but morally deficient society presents innumerable temptations and spiritual dangers for the unwary, and many—including quite a few who call themselves Christians—are tripped up in this manner. Those who foolishly consider themselves exempt from God's law place themselves in grave peril, for as Scripture warns, "A stubborn man will fare badly in the end, and he who loves danger will perish in it" (Sir. 3:25). At the same time, however, all who rely upon the mercy and providence of their heavenly Father will receive His blessings and protection. The words of the psalm must be our own:

In You, O Lord, I take refuge; let me never be put to shame. In Your justice rescue me, incline Your ear to me, make haste to deliver me! Be my rock of refuge, a stronghold to give me safety. You are my rock and my fortress; for Your Name's sake You will lead and guide me. You will free me from the snare they set for me, for You are my refuge (31:2-5).

God's Word is utterly reliable; the promises of this world are shallow and illusory, and it's our responsibility not to let ourselves be led astray by them. The great 19th century English cardinal and apologist Ven. John Henry Newman admonishes us, "You must either conquer the world or the world will conquer you. You must be either master or slave." May the graces and spiritual defenses Jesus shares with us through His Church one day allow all of us to share in His eternal triumph.

NOTES

[1]*Forty Dreams of St. John Bosco*, ed. by Fr. J. Bacchiarello, S. D. B. (TAN Books and Publishers, 1996), p. 206.

[2]Fr. Edgardo M. Arellano, *How to Win Your Spiritual Warfare* (Two Hearts Media Organization, Inc., 1994), p. 138.

[3]Mother Nadine Brown, *God's Armor* (Intercessors of the Lamb, 1998), p. 179.

[4]As St. Jerome notes, "The immoderate long fasts of many displease me, for I have learned by experience that the donkey worn out with fatigue on the road seeks rest at any cost. In a long journey, strength must be supported."

[5]On December 10, 1925, the Virgin Mary appeared to Sr. Lucia (the last surviving Fatima visionary) and said, "I promise to assist at the hour of death with all the graces necessary for salvation, those souls who, on the first Saturdays of five consecutive months, confess, receive Holy Communion, recite the Rosary and keep me company for fifteen minutes meditating on the fifteen mysteries of the Rosary with the intention of removing from (my Heart) these thorns" (namely, ingratitude and blasphemies against the Immaculate Heart).

[6]See Appendix B for a Consecration Prayer.

[7]See Appendix B for the format of the Divine Mercy Chaplet.

[8]*Diary* of St. Faustina, no. 129.

[9]*Diary* of St. Faustina, no. 93.

[10]Fr. Jeffrey J. Steffon, *Satanism—Is It Real?* (Servant Publications, 1992), p. 155.

[11]Joan Carroll Cruz, *Angels & Devils* (TAN Books and Publishers, 1999), pp. 223ff. As St. Anthony of Egypt stated, "Where the Sign of the Cross occurs, magic loses its power, and sorcery has no effect." Also, St. Ephrem advised, "Don't go out the door of your house till you have signed the cross. Whether in eating or in drinking, whether in sleeping or in waking, whether in your house or on the road, or again in leisure hours, don't neglect this sign—for there is no guardian like it. It will be for you like a wall in the forefront of all you do."

[12]Our Sunday Visitor's *Catholic Encyclopedia*, "Medals, Religious," p. 634.

[13]Rev. Albert Shamon, *Our Lady Teaches About Sacramentals and Blessed Objects* (The Riehle Foundation, 1992), p. 42.

[14]Cruz, op.cit. p. 234.

[15]Shamon, op.cit. pp. 2-3. One purpose of sacramentals, as Fr. Shamon explains, is to crush the devil's pride: "For God the Creator to take Satan on directly would dignify the fiend. Instead, God uses creatures, the weak things of the world, to confound the proud. Imagine mighty Lucifer being curbed by such weak and simple things as water, the Sign of the Cross, beads, a cloth Scapular" (p. 9).

Appendix A

How to Go to Confession

The first and most important thing to remember before receiving the Sacrament of Reconciliation (also known as Penance or Confession) is that *God is not seeking to condemn or punish you, but to forgive you and to embrace you with His love.*

Therefore, there is no reason for you to be afraid: if you are truly sorry for your sins (no matter how terrible or numerous they may be), the Lord's gracious forgiveness is *certain.* Also, the priest is not sitting in judgment; he himself, as a sinner in need of God's mercy, is happy to help you experience the Lord's forgiveness—and, of course, he can never reveal, in any manner, anything you mention in the confessional (so you can be completely honest with him).

Spend some time beforehand thinking about the sins you need to confess; perhaps an Examination of Conscience (available in various religious booklets) will be very useful. If you wish, you may also write down your sins and take that list into the confessional with you as a memory aid. It will be necessary to mention your serious or mortal sins specifically (as to the type of sin and the number of times you committed it); lesser or venial sins can be mentioned very briefly without any details.

It is not necessary to follow this (or any other) formula exactly; your intention to confess your sins and receive God's forgiveness is more important than the precise words used. (If you need to, you may also tell the priest you're unsure of how to make your confession, and he'll help you through the process.) Once in the confessional, you may follow these simple steps:

1. While making the Sign of the Cross, begin with these or similar words: "Bless me, Father, for I have sinned. It has been (number) months/years since my last confession. These are my sins."

2. Briefly mention your sins; include all your serious (mortal) sins, if any, and the number of times you committed them.

3. The priest will give you a penance (something to do as a sign of your gratitude for begin forgiven), and then ask you to say aloud an Act of Contrition. You may use this or a similar one, or, if you wish, one in your own words (in which you express your sorrow to God and promise to try to do better):

   My God, I am sorry for my sins with all my heart. In choosing to do wrong and in failing to do good, I have sinned against You Whom I should love above all things. I firmly intend, with Your help, to do penance, to sin no more, and to avoid whatever leads me to sin. Our Savior Jesus Christ suffered and died for us. In His Name, my God, have mercy.

4. The priest will then give absolution (the prayer of forgiveness), ending with the words "I absolve you from your sins in the Name of the Father, and of the Son, and of the Holy Spirit." As he says these words, make the Sign of the Cross.

5. Father will dismiss you by saying, "The Lord has freed you from your sins; you may go in peace." You may respond, "Thanks be to God." Following your confession, you may wish to spend some time praying in church. (This is especially suitable if you were given prayers to say as a penance.)

Appendix B

Prayers for Troubled Times

The Divine Mercy Chaplet

The Chaplet of Divine Mercy, which is ideally prayed at 3pm (but may be said at any time), uses the beads of an ordinary rosary. This format may be followed (saying the prayer either silently or aloud):

1. Begin with the Sign of the Cross.

2. Say one Our Father.

3. Say one Hail Mary.

4. Say the Apostles' Creed: "I believe in God, the Father almighty, Creator of heaven and earth; and in Jesus Christ, His only Son, our Lord; Who was conceived by the Holy Spirit, born of the Virgin Mary, suffered under Pontius Pilate, was crucified, died, and was buried. He descended to the dead. On the third day He rose again; He ascended into heaven, and is seated at the right hand of the God, the Father almighty. He will come again to judge the living and the dead. I believe in the Holy Spirit, the holy Catholic Church, the communion of saints, the forgiveness of sins, the resurrection of the body, and life everlasting. Amen."

5. On the large rosary bead at the start of each decade, say: "Eternal Father, I offer You the Body and Blood, Soul and Divinity of Your dearly beloved Son, our Lord Jesus Christ . . . in atonement for our sins and those of the whole world." (If several persons are praying the Chaplet aloud together, the leader says the first pray of the prayer, and the others respond with the second part. The same thing is true for #6 and #8 below.)

6. At each of the ten Hail Mary beads of the rosary, say "For the sake of His sorrowful Passion . . . have mercy on us and on the whole world."

7. Repeat this process for each of the remaining four decades.

8. After finishing the five decades, say the concluding doxology three times: "Holy God, Holy Mighty One, Holy Immortal One . . . have mercy on us and on the whole world."

9. (Optional:) Say the Closing Prayer: "Eternal God, in Whom mercy is endless and the treasury of compassion inexhaustible, look kindly upon us and increase Your mercy in us, that in difficult moments we might not despair nor become despondent, but with great confidence submit ourselves to Your holy will, which is love and mercy itself."

10. End with the Sign of the Cross.

The Rosary

Like the Divine Mercy Chaplet, the Rosary may be said—using ordinary rosary beads to help keep track of one's place—as part of a group, or alone (and, if alone, either aloud or silently). There are four different sets of five mysteries (the Joyful, the Luminous, the Sorrowful, and the Glorious), with each mystery corresponding to one decade (that is, one Our Father, ten Hail Marys, and one Glory Be). A Rosary normally consists of five decades, along with the opening and closing prayers (though more decades may be said, if desired). The following format may be used:

1. Begin with the Sign of the Cross.

2. Say the Apostles' Creed.

3. Say one Our Father (this corresponds to the large bead closest to the crucifix on the rosary).

4. Say three Hail Marys (corresponding to the three beads that follow).

5. Announce the first mystery, and say one Our Father.

6. Say ten Hail Marys.

7. End the first decade with a Glory Be, and then the prayer re-

quested by Our Lady at Fatima: "O my Jesus, forgive us our sins, save us from the fires of hell; lead all souls to Heaven, especially those in most need of Thy mercy."

8. Repeat this process (#5 – 7) for each of the remaining four decades.

9. Say the Hail Holy Queen: "Hail, Holy Queen, Mother of Mercy, our life, our sweetness, and our hope; to thee do we cry, poor banished children of Eve; to thee do we send up our sighs, mourning and weeping in this valley of tears. Turn, then, most gracious Advocate, thine eyes of mercy toward us, and after this, our exile, show unto us the blessed fruit of thy womb, Jesus. O clement, O loving, O sweet Virgin Mary! Pray for us, O holy Mother of God, that we may be made worthy of the promises of Christ."

10. End with the Sign of the Cross.

The Joyful Mysteries (Mondays & Saturdays)
1. The Annunciation (Lk. 1:26-38)
2. The Visitation (Lk. 1:39-56)
3. The Nativity of Jesus (Lk. 2:1-20)
4. The Presentation (Lk. 2:22-38)
5. The Finding of the Child Jesus in the Temple (Lk. 2:41-52)

The Luminous Mysteries (Thursdays)
1. The Baptism of Jesus (Mt. 3:13-17)
2. The Wedding Feast at Cana (Jn. 2:1-12)
3. The Proclamation of the Kingdom (Mk. 1:14-15)
4. The Transfiguration (Mk. 9:2-8)
5. The Institution of the Eucharist (Lk. 22:14-20)

The Sorrowful Mysteries (Tuesdays and Fridays)
1. The Agony in the Garden (Mt. 26:36-46)
2. The Scourging at the Pillar (Mt. 27:26)
3. The Crowning With Thorns (Mt. 27:28-29).
4. The Way of the Cross (Jn. 19:17-18)
5. The Crucifixion and Death of Jesus (Lk. 23:33-46)

The Glorious Mysteries (Wednesdays and Sundays)
1. The Resurrection (Mt. 28:1-10)
2. The Ascension (Lk. 24:50-51)
3. The Descent of the Holy Spirit (Acts 2:1-4)
4. The Assumption of Mary (Judith 13:18; Ps. 45:14-16)
5. The Coronation of Mary (Rv. 12:1)

Consecration Prayer to the Sacred Heart and Immaculate Heart

To consecrate the family, select a time when all can be present (ideally after all have attended Mass that day). Gather, if possible, before images of the Sacred Heart of Jesus and the Immaculate Heart of Mary, and recite this consecration prayer together:

Eternal Father, Your Divine Son became man to save and restore us all. He consecrated Himself for us, to assure our consecration in truth. Send Your Holy Spirit to consecrate me and my family to His Sacred Heart.

Jesus our Lord, King and Center of all hearts, Your Heart was the center of the Holy Family. Make it the center of my family, to make it holy too. I long to have my family united to You and to one another, living the truth in love. Mindful of Your promise to bless and heal families centered around Your Sacred Heart, we pray for family lives of peace and unity in You. Help us live by Your truth in the family of Your Church. We long for hearts like Yours, and families living in love, sharing Your mission of bringing the Father's love to every human being.

Mary ever Virgin, Mother of Jesus, by the Eternal Father's gift you are our Queen and Mother. We consecrate ourselves to your Immaculate Heart, that is ever centered in Jesus' Heart. May your motherly heart, His childhood guide, lead us to the truth and love that are His very Heart.

St. Joseph, head of the Holy Family, instill in us your love of the Divine Heart of Jesus, and the Immaculate Heart of Mary. Train us in the family life lived in your Holy Family. Guide our way home to the Holy Trinity, to share with your Holy Family the life of God forever. Amen.

(Apostleship of Prayer, 1992)

Prayer to St. Michael the Archangel

St. Michael the Archangel, defend us in battle; be our safeguard against the wickedness and snares of the devil. May God rebuke him, we humbly pray; and you, prince of the heavenly host, by the power of God, cast into hell Satan and all the evil spirits who prowl throughout the world seeking the ruin of souls.

Spiritual Warfare Prayer

Prayer to take authority on all that would block Christ's Lordship (to be said aloud or in a soft voice):

In the Name of Jesus, I take authority and I bind all power and forces in the air, in the ground, in the water, in the underground, in the netherworld, in nature, and in fire.

Lord Jesus Christ, You are the Lord over the entire universe and I give You the glory for Your creation. In Your Name, I bind all demonic forces that have come against us and our families, and seal all of us in the protection of Your Precious Blood that was shed for us on the Cross.

Mary, our Mother, we seek your protection and intercession with the Sacred Heart of Jesus for us and our families, and ask you to surround us with your mantle of love to discourage the enemy.

St. Michael and our guardian angels, come defend us and our families in battle against all the evil ones that roam the land.

In the Name of Jesus, I bind and command all powers and forces of evil, all spirits that are not of the Holy Spirit, to be bound right now to the foot of the Cross, away from us, our homes, and our lands. And we thank You, Lord Jesus, for You are a faithful and compassionate God. Amen.

Appendix C

Patron Saints for Frightened and Confused Catholics

The Church has always urged its members to cultivate a devotion to the saints—most especially the Blessed Virgin Mary, St. Joseph, and one's own favorites or patrons (based on baptismal names or occupations). The following saints might have special relevance for us in the 21st century (though these are only a few of the many who might be listed here):

St. Lucy is the patroness of persons with eye problems of a physical nature. However, many people today are *spiritually blind*—and so we might ask her help in seeing clearly what really matters in life, instead of letting ourselves be blinded by the false values of society.

While all seven Deadly Sins play a prominent role in American life today, *sexual temptations* or lust often take center stage. For that reason, it makes sense to seek the prayers and assistance of saints like Augustine and Margaret of Cortona—both of whom lived immoral lifestyles until being converted (and each of whom continued to struggle with sexual temptations, until overcoming them with the help of God's grace).

Technology is, for better or worse, an inescapable part of life in the 21st century—and so we might ask for the prayers and guidance of those saints who have some connection to this field. This would include St. Albert the Great, patron of scientists; the Archangel Gabriel, who is claimed as a patron by telecommunications workers and broadcasters; and St. Clare of Assisi, the considered the patroness of television viewers.

Along with technology, *bioethics* and *medicine* are major issues in contemporary American society—whether in terms of personal health, or in regard to our world's ever-more powerful "culture of death." Sts. Camillus de Lellis and John of God are patrons of hospitals and hospital workers. St. Elizabeth of Hungary, because of her work with the poor, is a patroness of nursing, unofficially along with, of course, Bl. Teresa of Calcutta (who, as Mother Teresa, was known throughout the world for her loving care of the desperately ill and dying). The patron saints of doctors are St. Luke (the "beloved physician" mentioned in Col. 4:14) and the brothers Sts. Cosmas and Damian, who combined the practice of medicine with a divinely-bestowed gift of healing. Their intercession is needed to ensure that modern medical technology is respectful of God's creation and truly ordered toward the well-being of His children.

Young people today face challenges and temptations to a degree that would have been unimaginable to earlier generations—involving peer pressure, rejection of authority, drug and alcohol abuse, the misuse of sex, spiritually corrosive music, occult activities, gang involvement, and so on. St. Dominic Savio and St. Maria Goretti are two relatively contemporary role models for young people today (especially in terms of resisting peer pressure and sexual impurity), but—in light of the almost overwhelming nature of these problems, and their (at least in part) diabolical origins—we would also do well to call upon the mighty spiritual intercession and protection of St. Michael the Archangel. As leader of the hosts of Heaven (and also as the patron of police officers), he has a special interest and power in helping preserve the young from moral corruption.

Is a *religious persecution* coming to our nation? If so, there are many role models who can show us how to remain true to Christ even at the risk of our lives, including St. John the Baptist, Sts. Perpetua and Felicity, St. Lawrence, a number of very young martyrs—including St. Agnes, St. Philomena, and St. Pancras—and several from the 20th century, such as Bl. Miguel Pro and St. Maximilian Kolbe. These and many other Catholic saints knew what it was like to experience persecution, and can help us stand firm if we too must one day face the prospect of giving up our lives in this world in order to attain the joys of eternity.

Are we facing a *desperate situation?* St. Jude, the patron of lost causes, is known for his powerful intercession in such cases. Is a *societal breakdown* a possibility? When the Western Roman Empire collapsed in the 5th century, it was St. Leo, the Bishop of Rome, and later one of his successors, St. Gregory the Great, who led the Church in helping restore order and rebuild civilization. Are we personally beset by fear, worry, or *depression?* St. Ignatius of Loyola was often depressed, but overcame this problem through divine grace. In this regard, the example of another always-popular saint can be helpful and encouraging: Thérèse of Lisieux, who demonstrated quiet humility and joyful resignation to the will of God in even the slightest things. These qualities are not popular in our world today—and it's precisely this which shows how greatly they're needed.

None of the saints faced exactly the same challenges we do in the 21st century (though there are surely men and women living among us right now who will one day be canonized by the Church); virtually all the saints, however, had serious obstacles to overcome on their journey to holiness—and some of them carried burdens far greater than anything we might imagine. These holy men and women from every age now look upon us from Heaven with immense love, and they stand ready—to the extent allowed by Divine Providence and human free will—to assist us through their prayers and intercession. Cultivating a devotion to the saints—these mentioned here, and many others as well—is one of the wisest and most spiritually profitable things we can do. There are many different prayers, novenas, and devotions for this purpose; the one which follows is an example of how we might invite any saint of our choosing to become a friend, confidant, and helper.

A Prayer for Saintly Assistance

Dear St. (name) , the world has changed greatly since you were alive on earth, and my life is very different from yours, but I believe you can relate to my hopes and fears, my burdens and my dreams. Indeed, you understand the world around me far better than I do, for you now see all things from the vantage point of eternity, and in the light of the Beatific Vision.

Because you now share in the fullness of holiness and wisdom, and have been made perfect in love and purity through God's grace, I confidently seek your assistance. May your intercession with the Holy Trinity obtain great blessings for all God's children in the world, including myself, my family, and my loved ones. May your prayers be a source of courage, strength, enlightenment, and peace of mind, along with an unyielding determination to live as faithful followers of Jesus, regardless of the cost. May your example inspire us to open our hearts ever more fully to the gifts of the Holy Spirit, thereby helping transform our world by doing all things for God's glory.

Dear St. (name) , may you and all the other saints and angels in the Kingdom of God look upon us with love and help us persevere in the ways of faith, so that one day we may join you, the Blessed Virgin Mary, and the entire heavenly court in praising the Most Holy Trinity, forever and ever.